H.A.P.P.Y

Holistic Approach to Personality, Psychometrics and You

Sreenidhi S.K., Tay Chinyi Helena,
Priyanka, Vaishali and Mayuri

INDIA • SINGAPORE • MALAYSIA

Notion Press

Old No. 38, New No. 6
McNichols Road, Chetpet
Chennai - 600 031

First Published by Notion Press 2019

ISBN 978-1-68466-191-6

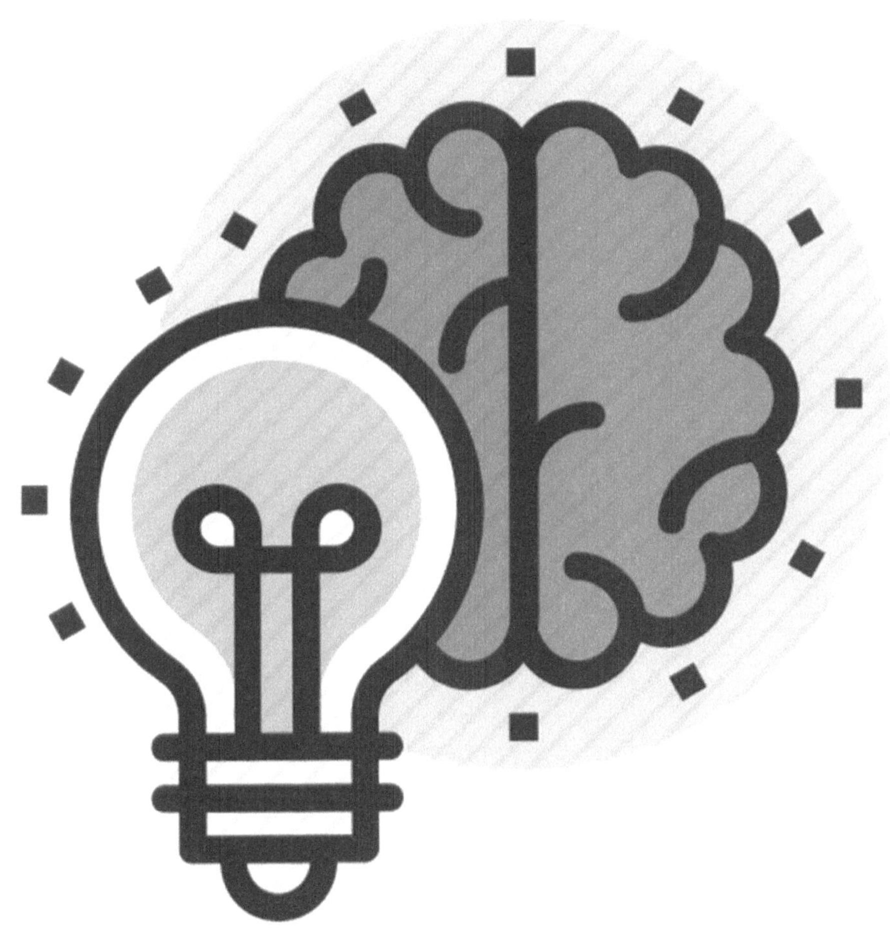

To be H.A.P.P.Y. is our birth-right. Amidst our daily hassles and problems, we often forget that through our decisions, we choose how our life goes. Every circumstance that we find ourselves in the middle of, is a circumstance we create, knowingly or unknowingly. While this may sound rather gloomy, the essential truth remains that we create our happiness.

To create happiness, we need to know where we want to go and how we want our happiness to look like. Once we have that figured out, the only thing that remains is paving the path towards it, and the first stepping stone of that path must be self-awareness.

Be aware of who you are, why you are that way, your patterns, your ticks, your strengths, your shortcomings. Know yourself and you will know how to make your envisioned happiness a reality. Know psychometrics, know your personality, know yourself!

Be H.A.P.P.Y.

Contents

Prelude That Alludes

Every person's life in this world is shaped by different influences. The use of psychometric assessments has grown into a multi-million-dollar industry. This book investigates how an objective battery of psychometric analysis of an individual's inherent strengths and capabilities ensure progress and growth in varied arenas of one's life.

The aim of the book is to explore the holistic approach by scientifically measuring the hidden strengths and discovering opportunities for self-progress and immediate growth possibilities through the Battery of Psychometric Analysis. The findings suggest that the background of psychological knowledge obtained was to help enable the individual to understand and make accurate choices in the course of one's life and career. It is established that one cannot depend on just one single psychometric assessment, as it is likely to open just one window of one's life. Hence, the **value of holistic approach** in applying the **Battery of Psychometric Assessments** is vital to open many influencing windows of an individual's life made up of – **Heredity, Upbringing, Environmental influences, Situational factors**, and more, as each one plays its own critical role.

This book reveals that the battery of multiple assessments serves as an objective tool in assisting people from various walks of life to gain awareness in optimizing and capitalizing on the strengths and powers of individuals/teams, to progress in life and career.

The Opening Statement

Through the course of this book, we will introduce multitudes of interesting revelations that are not new, just untold. To begin with, we would like to take you through how it all started and what it means.

The study of mind and behaviour – PSYCHOLOGY, is a behavioural science and psychologists study human behaviour by **observing, measuring, assessing** and arriving at **conclusions that are rooted in sound scientific methodology**. Psychological knowledge is applied in understanding and solving issues from different spheres of human activity, hereditary, environmental influences, human perceptions, attention, emotion, motivation, biological functioning of human mind, behaviour, personality, attitude and relationships.

From the Yesteryears Till Now

The word Psychometrics is formed from the Greek words for **mind** and **measurement**. Psychometric tests attempt to **objectively** measure aspects of individual's mental ability or personality.

As defined by National Council on Measurement in Education (NCME), psychometrics refers to **psychological measurement**. Generally, it refers to the field in psychology and education that is devoted to testing, measurement, assessment, and related activities. The tests explore intangible aspects such as **capabilities, aptitude, personality, behaviour patterns and such**.

The use of psychometrics as a science traces back to the late 19th century in Cambridge, between 1886 and 1889. The first laboratory dedicated to the science of psychometric test was set up in 1887 by James McKeen Cattell within the Cavendish Physics Laboratory, University of Cambridge.

However, personality testing only began in 1917 when Robert Woodworth developed the Personal Data Sheet, a simple yes-no checklist of symptoms that were used to screen the World War I recruits for psychoneurosis. This paved the way for other inventions like Minnesota Multiphasic Personality Inventory. Then, in the 1950s and 60s, the "Big Five" personality test was devised after a thorough analytical research to measure individual differences in personality which to this day remains a well-recognised personality traits model.

One part of the field is concerned with the objective measurement of skills, knowledge, abilities, attitudes, personality traits, and educational achievement. For example, some psychometric researchers have, thus far, concerned themselves with the construction and validation of assessment instruments such as questionnaires, tests, raters' judgments, and personality tests. Another part of the field is concerned with statistical research bearing on measurement theory (e.g., item response theory; intra-class correlation).

Practitioners are described as psychometricians, and they usually possess a specific qualification; most being psychologists with advanced graduate training. In addition to traditional academic institutions, many psychometricians work for the government or in human resources departments. Others specialize as learning and development professionals.

Psychometric assessments rose in popularity throughout the 20th century, and today a psychometric assessment is best described as a standardised assessment which looks at human behaviour and describes it with scores or categories. Today, we have access to a number of psychometric assessment tools which can be applied to **assess** and **develop people** from different walks of life.

Do We Really Need Psychometrics?

We all know that each one of us is a bundle of strengths and weaknesses. Each one of us needs an **objective evaluation** of our inherent strengths and capabilities as to ensure progress and growth. Weakness fixing prevents problems but **strength building speeds up success.**

Psychometrics is the emerging science adding immense value in **measuring the mind** of all its complexity. People from different walks of life from across the globe are resorting to gains from Psychometric Assessments and their interpretation. It is extremely useful in understanding the **different personalities, thinking attitudes, communication styles, behaviour patterns, inner motivations, likes & dislikes, conflicting choices, career preferences, leadership profiles, performance gaps, academic achievements, relationship challenges** and more.

- Psychometric assessments are often used by organizations and by individuals to assist in the **selection** and **development** of people

- The reason assessments are valuable is that they can uncover information that is not easily found by other traditional methods

- Assessments are good at uncovering if a person has the **potential to do a job** they have not yet had any experience in

- Well-designed psychometric assessments are objective and accurate **predictors** of individual behaviour and preferences

We are all interested in what makes people think and the understanding of psychometric assessments can help solve major people related issues in the society. The traditional methods of getting to know one's strengths and weaknesses carry the high risk of individual bias. Being subjective in nature, such outmoded methods are not comprehensive and hence, undermines the effectiveness of people performance.

Today, Behavioural Science of Psychology has made rapid advances in enabling **human understanding and appreciation of their potential.** Thereby, the benefits of the psychometric assessments, helps you become aware and can make use of it to **optimize human capital** by fully making use of **strengths and powers** to progress in life and career.

What Can You Read about People?

The two main types of psychometric assessments are:

- Ability Tests and Aptitude Tests

- Personality Tests & Interest Tests

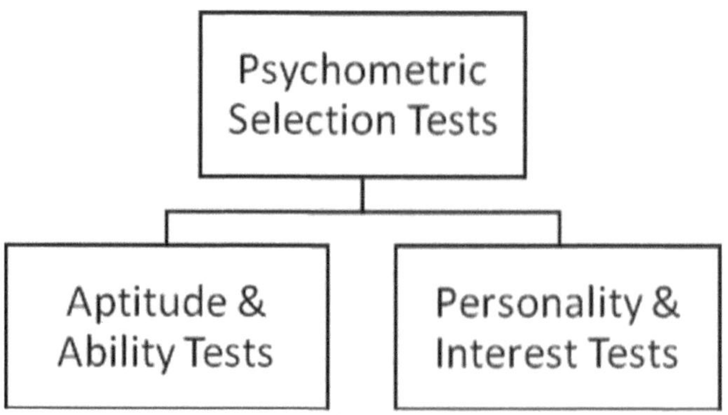

Ability tests are typically **timed tests** that measure a **specific ability or raw talent.** These tests are characterized by systematic ways of evaluating how people perform on tasks or react to different situations. Aptitude tests attempt to determine and measure your **ability to acquire** some specific **set of skills** [numerical reasoning ability, verbal ability], through **future training.** The tests assume that people differ in their special abilities and that these differences can be useful in predicting future achievements.

Aptitude tests use standardized methods of administration and scoring with the results quantified and compared with how others have done with the same tests.

Personality profiles are designed to measure a person's **personality preferences** and therefore, likely behaviours. Personality questionnaires differ from ability tests in that they look at 'style' rather than ability. In other words, they examine how you typically prefer to do things, such as the way you relate to others or how you approach tasks and solve problems.

Personality characteristics typically cover social confidence, anxiety levels and decision-making styles. Personality assessments are unbiased objective assessments and there are no right or wrong answers. Interest tests measure how people differ in their motivation, values, and opinions in relation to their interests.

Single and Battery of Assessments

The world of Psychometric analysis is made of several good instruments. But most of them are single instruments, meaning they are likely to throw light on only one aspect of life. Single instrument provides amazing insight into the personality providing tremendous input about their habits, preferences and strengths. But it still carries an incomplete and **partial view** of the individual.

There are many series of psychometric instruments that harness the power of psychology to help and understand others in building on their strengths to unlock their potential. Some focus on measuring a specific skill or aptitude, while others look to create a profile on a subject's particular trait. Here is an overview of some of the most widely-used psychometric instruments that have been relevant in the market.

The Psychometric Gems

Psychometric assessments are designed to measure a single factor (i.e. aptitude) or a variety of factors (i.e. skill level, motivation, etc.).

Some of the most popular psychometric assessments based on Jungian theory measure psychological preferences of how people perceive the world and make decisions. Questions are designed to determine whether the person taking the assessment is more extroverted or more introverted, whether he/she prefers to make decisions through thinking or feeling, whether he/she prefers to gather information through sensing or intuition, and whether he/she prefers to organize sense of the world through perceiving or judging.

While there are many advantages of these assessments, such as the results help people better understand their strengths, preferences and appreciate individual differences in others, learn to use their particular type to their own best advantage in dealing with others, become more effective communicators, there are a few disadvantages as well. For instance, **adequate knowledge of the theory** is necessary to administer and interpret the instrument. Simplicity of questions also encourages the idea that the typology itself is simple and static rather than multifaceted and dynamic, and people tend to get different results if they take the assessment more than once. To bridge these gaps, other personality assessments have been constructed.

FITS (Feeler, Intuitor, Thinker & Sensor Personality Style) is one of the **comprehensive assessment tool** built to bridge the gaps of other assessments. It is also based on **Carl Jung Personality Types** – Feeler, Intuitor, Thinker and Sensor and measures the personality types of individuals. This potent **Personality Style Assessment** helps discover the individual's **inherent personality style** and the scores measure the magnitude of each of the styles' influence, thereby recognizing that personality is multifaceted and not dichotomous, unlike its counterparts. Further, it also indicates the effective and ineffective sides to every personality style. It assists in developing oneself by using the right steps to enhance the strengths and provides valuable tips for recognizing personality types of others. The assessment is available in two versions, one for adults and one for children, with the statements in the assessments customised to suit the age group it is required to serve.

An awareness of one's personality style would help people understand their own **attitudes, thought patterns and behavioural tendencies**, enabling them to identify and manage their own responses to the environment. Further, knowledge about FITS would also facilitate an understanding of other individuals through their behaviours and preferences. This would **sensitise** them in their dealings with others, helping them **add value to relationships** and manage people efficiently.

Similarly, psychometric assessments have also been constructed on **four-quadrant behavioural model** based on the work of **William Moulton Marston Ph.D. (1893–1947)** to examine the behaviour of individuals in their environment or within a specific situation (otherwise known as environment) and focuses on the styles and preferences of such behaviour. **Dr. William Marston**, in the **1920s and 1930s**, explored the meaning of **normal human emotions** by relating how a person **perceives himself or herself** in **relation to the environment**, and their **likely behaviour in response to that environment.**

The two dimensions of Marston's model:

- The environment is perceived as favourable or unfavourable

- The individual perceives himself or herself as more or less powerful than the environment. In response to the environment, the individual either acts on or accommodates to that environment which is seen as either favourable or unfavourable.

These two principles **intersect to produce** four responses directed by emotions:

1. The **Dominant (controlling) response** acts on an environment perceived as unfavourable, while perceiving the self as more powerful

2. The **Inducement (convincing) response (later called influence)** acts on an environment perceived as favourable, while the self being more powerful than the environment

3. The **Submissive (consistent) response (later called steadiness)** acts on an environment perceived as favourable, owing to the self being perceived as less powerful

4. The **Compliance (conformity) response (later called conscientiousness)** acts on an environment perceived as unfavourable, while perceiving the self as less powerful

The tools based on this model describe an individual's place only on the 4 parameters: Dominance, Influence, Steadiness and Conscientiousness. However, individuals are profiled to fit one or **two prevalent types**, often not giving much importance to the types with low scores. Further, all possible combinations of primary and secondary types may not be accounted for. They also do not delineate the effective sides of low scores and ineffective sides of high scores. Further, often these days, assessments do not have time limits, allowing test takers to ponder upon questions, increasing the **probability of selecting socially desirable answers**.

4Cs (Controlling, Convincing, Conforming & Consistent Factors of Behaviour) is another tool based on the theory of **William Marston**, describing Controlling, Convincing, Conforming and Consistent responses of people. It measures the interplay of the four styles, taking into account every possible combination of scores, determining the magnitude of influence of each style on the individual's personality. Moreover, it considers the **possibility of having a balanced personality style.**

The assessment describes **behavioural traits, communication styles** as well as **intrinsic motivators** and **stressors**. It also throws light on individuals as **people oriented or task oriented**, reflecting the style by which they will get work done. It also helps find out if an individual is '**Active or Passive**' in their approach to work and life. Further, it also indicates the effective and ineffective sides to every personality style. The assessment is also available in two versions, one for adults and one for children, with the statements in the assessments customised to suit the age group it is required to serve.

Knowledge about 4Cs facilitates an understanding of self and others, helping in identifying the differences between each other's styles. This enables people to **flex their styles to communicate effectively, improving interpersonal interaction**. It also helps identify how people complement each other's strengths and weaknesses, thereby investing in mutually beneficial relationships.

Instruments that measure personality traits have also been created based on Cattell's theory, Eysenck's theory and such. Competencies are derived from the traits measured. However, the questions of these assessments may not necessarily be work-related, and are **interpreted for various contextual requirements** instead, such as recruitment and succession planning.

PPC 20 (People Performance Competency 20) is a tool based on the work of well recognized psychologists & management specialists like **Boyatziz, Kirton, McClelland and Mintzberg**. It measures **20 traits contextual to work, under 5 Meta Performance Competencies**. It gives a wholesome picture about the individual, assessing various behavioural factors affecting performance at work.

Quantifying these people performance competencies would help an individual **recognise their strengths and limitations**. Measuring where they stand on a particular skill/ability for their roles/responsibilities, and where they want to be, would help **identify gaps**, enabling people to **chart out individual development plans to bridge the same**. Competency mapping can be done to determine person-job fit for recruitment, succession planning, behavioural interventions and such. The assessment also takes into account the negatives and positives of each score, be it low, ideal or uncharacteristically high, i.e. overstrength.

CPA (Communication Pattern Analysis) based on **Eric Berne's Transactional Analysis** provides an insight into **individual response patterns in interpersonal communications**. This assessment assesses the impact of various factors like **upbringing, environmental influences** etc. that **establishes certain communication habits** of the individual. Since effective communication is an essential component of organizational success, whether it is at the interpersonal, inter-group, intra-group, organizational, or external levels, this assessment would help individuals deal and communicate with others at work and off work by utilising the best response mode or combination of the four response modes (**Advise, Criticise, Empathy and Search**) to achieve optimal results.

BPA (Behaviour Pattern Analysis) based on **B.F. Skinner's** theory illustrates **environmental influences** on an individual by **identifying and comparing behaviour patterns in variable situations**. Since human behaviour is the collection of behaviours influenced by culture, attitudes, emotions, values, ethics, authority, rapport, persuasion, coercion and/or genetics, this tool brings to light the manner of behaviour across situations. It provides a balanced view of behaviour of an individual.

The **VAK (Visual, Auditory, Kinesthetic Learning Style)** learning styles model developed by **Fernald, Keller, Orton, Gillingham, Stillman, Montessori and Neil D Fleming**, provides a simple way to **explain and understand one's own learning style (and learning styles of others)** to assess the preferred learning modes, and most importantly, to incorporate **learning methods** and **experiences** that match **one's strengths and preferences**. There are no right or wrong learning styles. The fact is that there are different types of learning styles that suit different people. This assessment is widely applicable to different kinds of population from students to adults.

CARS (**C**oncrete, **A**bstract, **R**andom and **S**equential Learning **Preferences**) model developed by **Anthony F. Gregorc**, provides insights into how individuals **gather and assimilate information**. It is of immense value as awareness into such aspects can be utilized towards building on their natural learning preferences. Knowing how you learn and how you relate to the world can help you make smarter choices. It provides a better chance of avoiding problematic situations and helps understand as to how differently people learn.

The **PRSE** (**P**articipating, **R**eflecting, **S**tructuring and **E**xperimenting Learning) model developed by **David Kolb**, assesses the approach (Participating, Reflecting, Structuring and Experimenting) an individual takes to **organize and internalize information**. This provides an objective analysis to understand the means by which one organizes new learning. It helps to understand the strengths and weaknesses in learning, to discover how to learn best and facilitates best performance that boosts confidence.

The **Multiple Intelligence Assessment (MI)** based on the **theory of multiple intelligence** developed by **Howard Gardner** provides **nine different potential pathways to learning.** All human beings possess all nine intelligences in varying degrees. These nine intelligences may operate in **consort** or **independently** from one another. To achieve an edge in learning, an individual can **leverage** that intelligence where he/she shows strength so as to **develop** in the area where they may have a challenge.

The **LEAP** (**L**eaders **E**ffective **A**ptitude **P**rofile Assessment) profile based on the different leadership styles provides **awareness of personal leadership style** and its implications to develop leadership skills and **flex leadership techniques** according to **situational demands.** The insight provided by this assessment acts as an underpinning for comprehensive and balanced leadership effectiveness. This tool is extensively used as a prelude to leadership skill development. It determines if leaders **lead by defining goals and organizing systems and resources to** minimize wastages and maximize predictability. It also assesses if they actively provide feedback to develop people, lead by providing a vision of future opportunities or **by example and personal experience in the chosen field of expertise.**

CRP (**C**hange **R**esponse **P**rofile Assessment) aims to determine concerns people have when change is implemented in their environment. It helps in **identifying** and **responding** accordingly to the **worries, attitudes,** and **perceptions of people** as they **deal with the challenges of changing** the way they work. It also provides early indication of reasons for resistance within the organisation and offers insight into what exactly concerns an individual regarding the change. It also facilitates the management's understanding of apprehensions and challenges faced by their workforce to deal with change effectively.

The Power Can Be Vested in All of You

Entrepreneurs/Directors

To succeed in business, you need the right people to support your vision and value. The worst threat for any entrepreneur today is to **hire people who don't fit in** to the job or the culture. The résumé looks great and the cover letter is impressive indeed; concentrating more on the technical competencies, many firms tend to overlook the behavioural competencies, which hold a lot of significance.

As an entrepreneur/director, psychometric assessments are helpful to:

- Identify the person whose beliefs align with the organisational vision and mission

- Gauge if people strategies are aimed at nurturing attitudes that help create the envisioned organisational culture

- Customise developmental plans and propose learning curves based on innate potentials of the workforce

- Identify high potentials and optimise their strengths to build an efficient leadership pipeline

Succession Planning, the Story... Your Connect!

Common as conundrums are, a company was weighing two employees at the managerial level in the department of Accounts for the position of Deputy General Manager of Accounts and Costing department. At the precipice of making a decision with significant impact on not only the workforce, but the organisation' future, the decision had to be infallible. The candidates were to be assessed on competencies and abilities such as critical analysis, maintenance of records, maintaining relationships with stakeholders, and such to suggest the best suitable candidate for the promotion.

The decision was crucial to the company, and they wanted to be absolutely sure of the candidate. They needed to understand if the candidate would be able to perform now as well as rise to future responsibilities. Hence, to get a broad-gauged understanding, the candidates were instructed to take up a Battery of 4 Assessments to understand their inherent personality (FITS), the influence of environment (4Cs), communication patterns (CPA) and the current competencies (PPC20). In addition to the assessment interpretations, skills required for the role were referred to from the Job Description and the background details of both the potential candidates such as their current key responsibility areas were considered to conclude the recommended candidate.

*Hooked? Find the whole story in the Annexure!

Managers

Managers play a key role in **influencing people's commitment level** and **retention**, therefore understanding what motivates people becomes a critical factor. Good interpersonal relationship skills help the manager facilitate better performance, which is likely to enhance job satisfaction and increase motivation.

Psychometric assessments can help managers with:

- Using strengths and skills to create opportunities for growth

- Coping with one's weaknesses to deal with possible threats

- Developing one's leadership potential and facilitating their career growth

- Enhancing interpersonal dynamics and building stronger teams

- Enabling team members to flex their communication style to suit specific differences and needs

- Enhancing productivity and performance at all levels

- Getting people to develop the right competency required for the job

---

Team Profiling, the Story... Your Connect!

An executive coach and trainer wanted to gauge how a team of 6 people from an organisation functioned collaboratively as leaders. While each leader was highly qualified on their own, the client wanted to understand what the team members' strengths and challenges were and identify how each member's skills could supplement another's shortcoming.

The team had taken a Battery of 4 assessments – FITS, 4Cs, CPA and PPC20. The battery gauged their innate potentials, behaviours, motivators, stressors, communication patterns and current competencies. The individual scores were consolidated and interpreted according to nine parameters provided by the client. The nine parameters were: Process, Strategic Direction, Relationships, Team Work, Customer Orientation, Commitment to Purpose, Internal Communication, External Communication and Resilience. The strengths and challenges faced by the team for each parameter were delineated and recommendations were made to bridge the gaps identified.

Hooked? Find the whole story in the Annexure!

HR Recruitment Consultant

Psychometric assessments could be used to **improve placement success** and hence, gain customer confidence which would mean – more business. It is a way for employers to assess the intelligence, competency and personality. Recruiters use the results from these tests to determine whether the candidate would be a **suitable match** for the organisation to which they are applying.

Psychometric tools help recruiters with:

- Matching the right candidate for the right job

- Less guesswork in placing candidates on the job

- Increased placement success to reduce cost of rehiring

- Positive client's perceptions of one's hiring ability

- Enhance their credibility by using scientific methods to screen and shortlist candidates

> ## Recruitment, the Story... Your Connect!
>
> In a time where talent with determination is hard to spot, the Managing Director of an automotive company faced a fortunate confusion of deciding the best candidate out of 3 highly eligible candidates.
>
> To alleviate the pressure of making a costly mistake, a battery of 5 assessments were proposed for the 3 candidates. The scores from the psychometric assessments were aligned with the job description, along with the resume of the candidates. This provided a comprehensive understanding of the indicators of the candidates' probable behaviours and responses in various situations, which was then measured against the expected behaviours and competencies mentioned in the job description.
>
> The best candidate was then identified based on the degree of match between the candidate's profile and the job description, organisational needs and culture.
>
> *Hooked? Find the whole story in the Annexure!

Sales Professionals

Sales personnel who are expected to **build lasting relationships** with their customers have the benefit of high success rates. Sales people make use of psychometric assessments to enable themselves to **understand each customer's buying style** and **change their selling style** accordingly since 'One size fits all' approach does not work in Sales.

Psychometric tools help Sales personnel with:

- Understanding their own personality and communication styles

- Gauge the personality and buying behaviours of others

- Identify effective communication strategies to hone their convincing skills

- Expedite success in negotiation situations

- Devise customised impactful approaches that drive buy-in

Coaches/Mentors

People are different and respond differently to situations. Work place anxiety, personal worries, insecurities, inferiority complex, conflict, values, beliefs and expectations need to be dealt differently based on people's behavioural style that are bound to be different for different people. Psychometric Assessments provide an insight to the client's personality and pave the **right coaching pathway to suit different personality styles** to **empower people** and prepare them to deliver expected results.

Psychometric tools aid **Coaches/Mentors to:**

- Gauging the innate potential and untapped abilities of people to motivate and inspire them to question their limits, promoting their advancement

- Promoting a holistic understanding of clients to customize the coaching approach and help empower them

- Enhance their ability to provide constructive feedback objectively based on the individuals' personality pattern to align with his or her career or life goals

- Gauge the factors that are likely to inspire them, and be an enabler to get them to put the best foot forward to gain against all odds

- Equip the clients to identify and nurture their intrinsic motivations to initiate their personal development

Coaching, the Story... Your Connect!

A global production-based industry had acquired a local manufacturing company which was unable to thrive in the volatile business conditions. This industry's agenda was to unite the local employees and their own employees to bring about a unified culture. A new CEO was appointed to bring about cohesiveness among the employees who were used to their own ways and were part of separate organisational cultures. The expectations from the CEO was that he/she would be able to bring harmony between these different personalities and lead the newly formed company towards a unified vision. The position thus required a leader who can build and maintain effective relations and follow strategic planning to bring in profits.

The candidate was instructed to take up a Battery of 5 Assessments to understand inherent personality (FITS), the influence of environment (4Cs), communication (CPA) and behaviour patterns (BPA) and the current competencies (PPC20) of the individual. As part of the process intervention, the candidate also underwent intensive reflective sessions with a coach and change agent, who had previously interacted with the organisation to understand their culture, vision and mission. This allowed the coach to bring about optimized success for the individual as well as the organization.

*Hooked? Find the whole story in the Annexure!

Career Counsellors

Psychometric assessments enable professionals to **match the student's personality style** and **talents** with **right career** options. The **career mapping** due to psychometrics help the students to discover their innate natural talents and work by using their strengths for quicker progress and better performance. The tool can also help individuals who feel stuck in their current jobs and are seeking to venture into a different field but are unsure about which arena to pursue.

Psychometric tools enable career counsellors to:

- Gauge the innate potentials, aptitudes, intelligence and learning styles of students to create effective learning methodologies

- Identify curricula that are perfect for students based on the congruency between the curriculum and the student's potential and personality

- Match an individual's personality, abilities and interest with relevant career paths

- Conduct root cause analysis of underperformance in academics or work and curate strategies to facilitate improvement

- Facilitate interventions for teachers and professors to align teaching pedagogies with their class's learning style

- Guiding people undergoing midlife crisis, by understanding their personality types

Career Mapping, the Story... Your Connect!

A 21-year-old student, who had completed his/her bachelor's in Business and Management, faced the challenge of choosing a career. While he/she had gained work experience by working with event companies and various other MNCs as sales personnel as well as a host/hostess, the confusion in his/her mind was unyielding. With all his/her friends confident about what they wanted to do, this individual was facing immense stress. To decide on a career, he/she wanted to gauge his/her strengths and challenges, and depending on them, determining a career path that would suit him/her the best.

To assist the candidate, he/she was instructed to take up a Battery of 4 Assessments to understand his/her inherent personality (FITS), the influence of environment (4Cs), learning style preference (CARS) and Multiple Intelligences (MI) as this would help choose the right career that suits him/her.

*Hooked? Find the whole story in the Annexure!

Family/Marriage Counsellors

Psychometrics is a significant tool for understanding human behaviour. They can help identify the **cause of interpersonal issues** and find **ways to resolve** the same. It can also **deepen parental understanding** of their children and enable improved and easier way to deal with them. Further, when children are grown up and are starting to look at career choices, the assessments help in identifying potential options that result in far better performance.

- Using the psychometric results to help individuals understand partners to facilitate harmonious relationships

- Discovering personality differences between partners/spouses and determining how to leverage the differences to enhance the relationship

- Identifying the interactional pattern of both the spouses

- Guiding parents to understand their personality and behaviour and its impact on their children

- Understand their child's learning style to enhance his/her academic and overall performance

- Helping parents understand what the child needs rather than assuming or believing what their needs are

Trainers and L&D Professionals

Psychometric assessments and interpretation add immense value to the **effectiveness of training programs or processes**. Participants can realistically connect to their individual scores and past behaviours, encouraging themselves to reflect and introspect. The interpretation is a powerful tool to provoke the change in their thinking, attitudes and their behaviours. The Psychometric assessments and interpretations act as enablers to instil lasting changes in people as one witnesses a clear transfer of learning from workshop to workplace.

Psychometric tools enable trainers and learning & development professionals to:

- Conduct training need analysis by understanding individual strengths and shortcomings

- Identify gaps in performance and determine the reasons behind the same

- Expedite performance by tapping into the hidden strengths and developing the same

- Enable others to work towards bringing about a change in their behaviours

- Create customised intervention modules based on the collective potential of people as well as the organisational needs

Organisational Behaviour Profiling, the Story... Your Connect!

An organisation was facing a common issue with their entire workforce – the lack of ownership, accountability and responsibility. At the edge of a 'perform or perish' situation, something had to be done. They felt that their workforce was used to set ways, going about their routine operations and did not have a futuristic outlook. This hampered the speed of progress towards materialising the organisation's collective vision. Based on detailed discussions with the organisation's leaders, behavioural interventions were designed to attain the particular objectives of fostering ownership, accountability and responsibility. As part of the process intervention, the participants had taken two psychometric assessments, FITS and PPC. This enabled them to gauge the gap between their potentials and current performance. The scores of all the participants across batches were collated and studied and it was found that the scores corroborated with the existing situation. Recommendations were made based on the gap gauged between the potential and performance of the teams as well.

*Hooked? Find the whole story in the Annexure!

Let's Talk about
Metrics – Psychometrics

Since the individual assessments can be challenged to provide a holistic approach of human understanding, what is the right solution?

While the industry has been heavily reliant on singular psychometric tools, as they are easily available and cost effective, they do not provide a holistic picture of an individual's personality. However, this is not to say that single assessments are ineffective by themselves. As standalone tools, they do serve specific purposes. However, they may be found lacking when one desires to understand multiple facets of an individual, such as how he/she would communicate or behave in certain situation, whether or not he/she has nurtured the innate potential within them and such.

The world of Psychometrics has opened up the new **holistic dimension** into **understanding people's attitude, beliefs, values, competency and personality**. Based on the extensive work of eminent scientists, increasing number of professionals have practically experienced the full power of **Multiple Psychometric Gems** – a Battery of assessments which enable people to develop the belief in the most **rational** and **logical system** in gauging oneself and **harnessing one's true potential**. This becomes the right start in measuring gaps between performance and potential towards success.

These tools are specifically designed to give a **kaleidoscopic insight** into behaviours, attitudes, motivation and perceptions which have a major impact on the bottom line performance across profiles. The outcomes also offer actionable insights into areas of improvement.

Every individual is a bundle of strengths and weaknesses, but only a few make use of their inherent strengths. The vast majority of people, unknowingly and unintentionally, tend to use their weaknesses and end up on the losing side in their career, life and relationships.

The Battery of assessments provides a **psychometric horoscope** for the test takers that identifies their innate untapped potentials, unexplored strengths and capabilities, empowering them with self-awareness and an opportunity for self-growth and development. Varied areas of improvement are also identified and addressed. Indeed, the multiple assessments combine to form powerful tools for being a Strength Finder and Enabler.

The Battle of Single V/S Battery of Assessments (BAT)

1. **FITS:**

   Scores on FITS can range from 10 to 40. The scores across all four types should amount to 100.

   - *Primary Score(s) (P):* The highest score of the person, indicating that they would display the primary personality characteristics most often.

   - *Secondary Score(s) (S):* Any score(s) within a range of 4 from the primary score. For example, if Primary is 29, Secondary scores could be 25 to 28. The secondary personality characteristics will be displayed quite often as well.

   - *Median Score(s) (M):* Any score apart from the primary or secondary scores that falls within the range of 22.5 to 27.5. The person would display these characteristics when the situation demands it.

   - *Balanced Score(s):* People may have fairly balanced scores across the 4 styles. In this case, they display characteristics of all four styles to a moderate extent. However, being pulled by the different styles, they might experience confusion.

Table 1: Representing the FITS personality assessment scores of Mr. X

Feeler	Intuitor	Thinker	Sensor
28.5	23	21.5	27

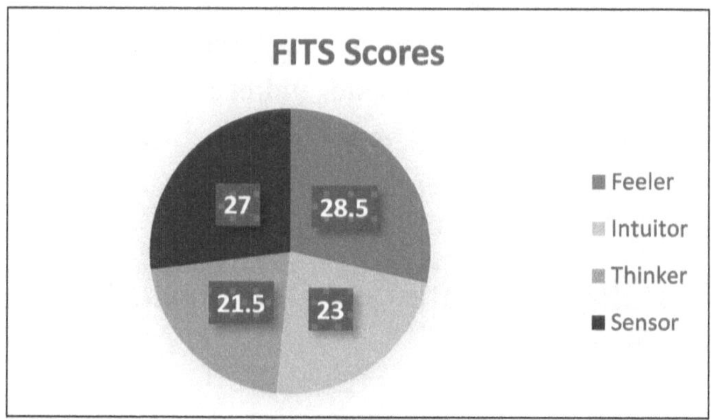

Figure 1: Representing the FITS personality assessment scores of Mr. X

From table 1 and graphical representation 1, it is evident that by picking up emotional cues from people, the subject exhibits the inherent strength to **understand people, as indicated by his/her primary Feeler score.** He/She tends to be **in tune with** his/her **moods, feelings** and is **sensitive to the emotional needs of others.** Thus, he/she comes across as a **warm, friendly** and **considerate** person; often **enjoying the company of people.** He/she is likely to be **more concerned about people's reactions** than objective reality. Hence, may find oneself **doing things he/she may not like,** in order to gain others' **approval.** Furthermore, he/she tends to be **sentimental,** holding emotional attachments to specific objects, situations and events. This inclination may **cloud his/her ability to take objective decisions** at times.

His/her secondary **Sensor** score indicates that he/she is also **inherently a goal-driven individual** with the potential to **accomplish** tasks and get things done on time and as per the expected standards. The subject may come across as a **hardworking** and **determined** individual. He/she may have **hands on style** in doing his/her work and is likely to be **pragmatic** in his/her **approach**. Being **action-oriented**, he/she would be comfortable **working** at a **fast pace** and is likely to enjoy investing his/her efforts in tasks that **yield** results he/she can see.

Since he/she is **engrossed** in the world of **emotions** and **action,** generating **original ideas** and **out-of-the box thinking** may **not be appealing** to him/her, as indicated by the **median Intuitor score**. Further, placing importance on people and the relationships he/she holds, **approaching tasks** and **processing of information** in an **organized way** may be challenging for him/her, as expressed by the **low Thinker score**. He/she may also **find it hard** to meticulously **plan** his/her **activities.** **Weighing the pros and cons of ideas,** alternatives and situations **may not come naturally to him/her**, hence, **logical analysis** may be a challenge.

2. **4Cs:**

   Interpretation of scores obtained on 4C's is the same as FITS:

   - *Primary Score(s) (P):* The highest score of the person, indicating that they would display the primary personality characteristics most often.

   - *Secondary Score(s) (S):* Any score(s) within a range of 4 from the primary score. For example, if Primary is 29, Secondary scores could be 25 to 28. The secondary personality characteristics will be displayed quite often as well.

   - *Median Score(s) (M):* Any score apart from the primary or secondary scores that falls within the range of 22.5 to 27.5. The person would display these characteristics when the situation demands it.

   - *Balanced Score(s):* People may have fairly balanced scores across the 4 styles. In this case, they display characteristics of all four styles to a moderate extent. However, being pulled by the different styles, they might experience confusion.

Table 2: Representing the 4Cs personality assessment scores of Mr. X

Controlling (C1)	Convincing (C2)	Conforming (C3)	Consistent (C4)
27	22	27	24
Active Initiator (C1+C2)	**Passive Responder (C3+C4)**	**Task Oriented (C1+C3)**	**People Oriented (C2+C4)**
49	51	54	46

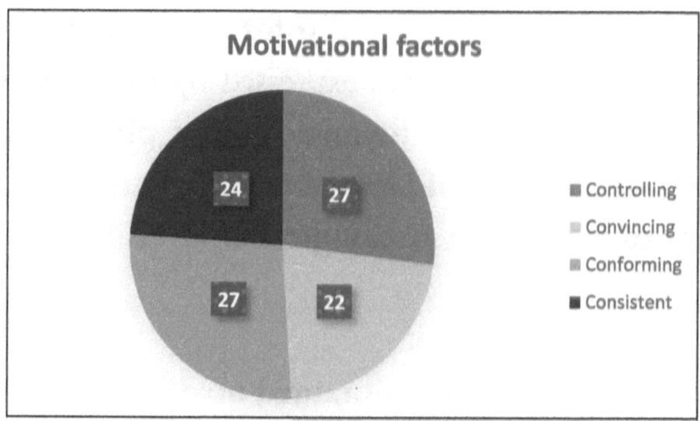

Figure 2.1: Representing the 4Cs personality assessment scores of 'X'

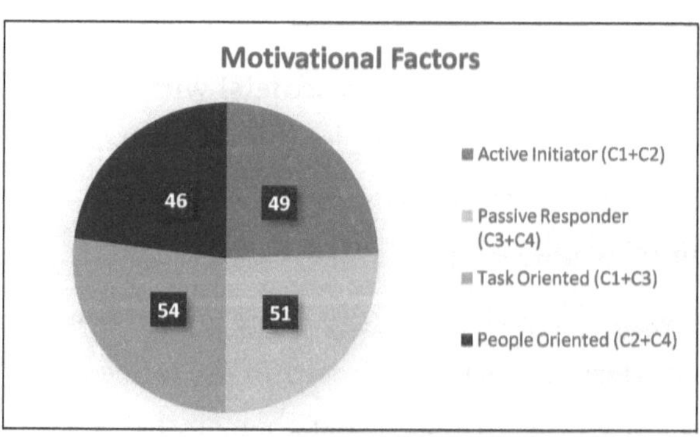

Figure 2.2: Representing the 4Cs personality assessment scores of 'X'

From table 2 and graphical representation 2.1, a **high Controlling** score indicates that the individual is likely to be **driven to achieve results**. The subject would tend to **enjoy challenging tasks, takes charge and deal with hurdles** that may come in his/her way to achieve targets.

The subject's **competitive spirit** guides him/her to seek opportunities for individual accomplishment and is often motivated by the level of difficulty or complexity involved in the work.

Further, as indicated by the **equally high Conforming score**, the subject seeks **accuracy** and **predictability** in results, and is likely to prefer working with **established methodologies**. He/she is likely to be comfortable to work within a **structured environment** and would strive to **meet the defined standards of quality**. He/she tends to respect authority and hence, is likely to abide by the rules and **adhere to policies** and regulations. With the need to be correct, he/she is likely to seek reassurance from others to confirm if he/she is going in the right direction.

As indicated by the **Consistent score**, which is a **secondary score**, the subject is likely to **value relationships** and tends to **avoid interpersonal conflicts**. When faced with **contradictions** and conflicts, he/she may take **support of policies** and conventions to **resolve it objectively**. Further, the subject is also able to handle long term assignments and will continue to work until the completion of the same.

Being **balanced on the Active and Passive initiator** scores, the subject is likely to **take charge when necessary**. Further, to achieve goals, he/she would use available resources judiciously as well as explore the environment to procure additional resources. Displaying a preference towards tasks than people, the subject tends to focus on timely task completion and attainment of results that meet the standards of quality.

BAT 2 Discussion: FITS & 4Cs

Feeler	Intuitor	Thinker	Sensor
28.5	23	21.5	27
Controlling (C1)	Convincing (C2)	Conforming (C3)	Consistent (C4)
27	22	27	24
Active Initiator (C1+C2)	Passive Responder (C3+C4)	Task Oriented (C1+C3)	People Oriented (C2+C4)
49	51	54	46

As indicated by the FITS scores, the individual is a primary Feeler, secondary Sensor, median Intuitor and low Thinker. This indicates that he/she has the **inherent potential to pick up on emotional cues** and **respond in a sensitive manner**. The subject is also goal driven by nature and has an **action-oriented approach to tasks**. The **Controlling score**, indicating that he/she is willing to tackle challenges confidently to overcome barriers and persevere, also **corroborate his Sensor score**. He/she also has the ability to approach a situation from multiple angles and **generate different methods of completing tasks** when the situation demands. However, as indicated by the **high Conforming scores**, the **individual is unlikely to do this**, preferring to stick to the established as it provides a sense of security.

Though his/her **Thinker score is the lowest**, he/she has **developed the ability to work in a structured and organized manner, delve into details and ensure accuracy**. This is evidently **learned behaviour as the innate potential to do so is low**. Moreover, while he/she is **primarily a feeler**, his/her **people orientation is uncharacteristically low**. This indicates environmental influences rendered him to adopt behaviours contradictory to his inherent nature in order to adapt. It also indicates that his/her true potentials were not allowed to develop by a thwarting environment. Both of the aforementioned inferences were drawn as a result of linking the scores of the two assessments, as the two in isolation mention contradictory traits.

3. **CPA:**

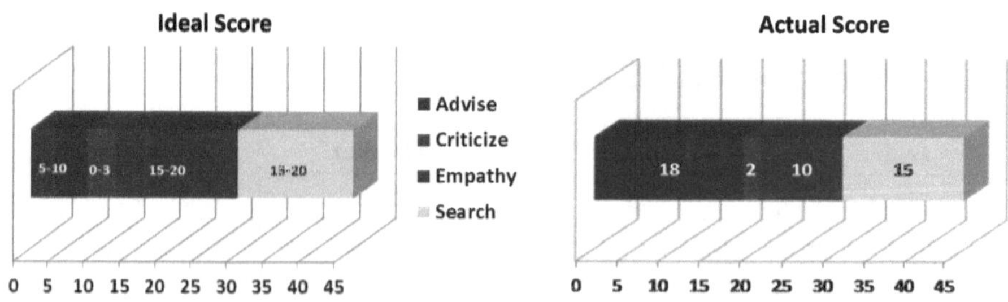

Figure 3.1: Representing the Ideal and the Actual Scores of the Communication Pattern of 'X'

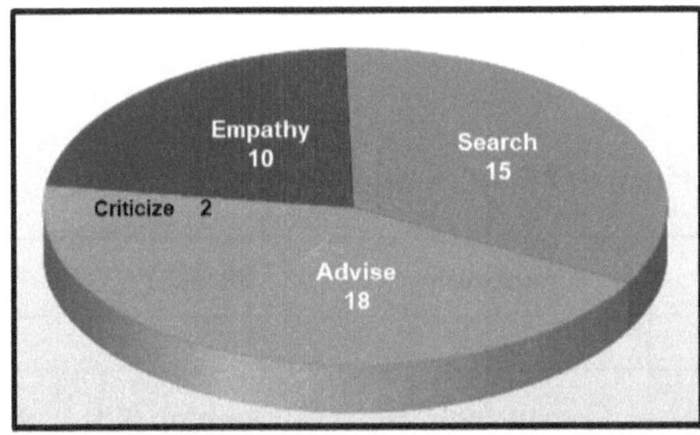

Figure 3.2: Representing the Communication Pattern Scores of 'X'

From the above graph, it is clear that the subject has scored **18, 15, 10** and **2** in the **Advising, Searching, Empathizing** and **Criticizing Communication Patterns,** respectively. As an **individual** who exhibits a **desire to help**, the subject tends to **offer suggestion or solutions** to people to guide them regarding what to do. He/she is likely to look at the brighter side of things and focus on appreciating others. While the subject would **recognize mistakes**, he/she tends to offer advice on how to **make amends** rather than calling out the faults, as indicated by a **high Advise** and **ideal Criticize** score.

To figure out the **root of the issue** the other person is facing, the subject is likely to **ask various questions,** as implied by the **Search** score which lies in the ideal scores bracket. This helps the subject gain an overall picture of the problem, enabling him/her to suggest solutions and avoid misdiagnosis of issue. However, he/she **may not** try to **understand** it from the **point of view of the person** facing it, as indicated through the **low Empathy** score. Although offering guidance is beneficial, a significant focus on the same may lead to a dependency in relationships, affecting overall productivity when the individual is unavailable to provide assistance.

Further, the subject's tendency to focus on the solution may divert him/her from listening to what the others have to say. Understanding and considering the person's perspective would provide context and clarity into the root cause of the problem. In addition, it also prevents him/her from jumping to conclusions.

BAT 3 Discussion: FITS, 4C's and CPA

Feeler	Intuitor	Thinker	Sensor
28.5	23	21.5	27
Controlling (C1)	Convincing(C2)	Conforming (C3)	Consistent (C4)
27	22	27	24
Active Initiator (C1+C2)	Passive Responder (C3+C4)	Task Oriented (C1+C3)	People Oriented (C2+C4)
49	51	54	46
Advise	Criticize	Empathy	Search
18	2	10	15

As indicated by the FITS scores, the individual is a primary Feeler, secondary Sensor, median Intuitor and a low Thinker. The scores indicate that he/she is likely to be charged and enthusiastic to take on challenges. He/she has the ability to build relationships easily and get along with others. His/her high feeler scores indicate that he/she has the innate ability to relate to people and pick up emotional cues, helping him/her **respond in a considerate manner**. However, as **indicated by the Empathy scores**, when approached with issues he/she **may not actually try to listen to others** and **understand their perspectives.**

Though he/she is a Feeler, his/her people orientation is low which could be because of environmental influence. Being Task oriented, he/she tends to give importance to task completion. He/she **asks for additional information to get to the root of the problem** and proceeds to **provide suggestions and solutions** instead, as indicated by his/her **Advise** score. This corroborates with his/her Conforming and Controlling scores, which indicates that he/she has the ability to lead and overcome barriers and is likely to rely on established procedures do so. The subject is likely to **advocate the use of tried and tested methods.** His Controlling score also indicates that he/she prefers work to be done in a certain manner and aims for precision and quality as exhibited through conforming scores, he/she is inclined to take an advisory stance.

Having a high score on Advise also shows that he/she may **recommend solutions** to others out of his/her genuine desire to help, which also lies in alignment with the high Feeler score. However, it is likely that this individual's **high Advise score** is being **derived from his Task-Oriented nature**, as the **empathy** score is rather low and consistent is a median score, as opposed to his/her scores on **task orientation** and a secondary **sensor** score.

4. **PPC20:**

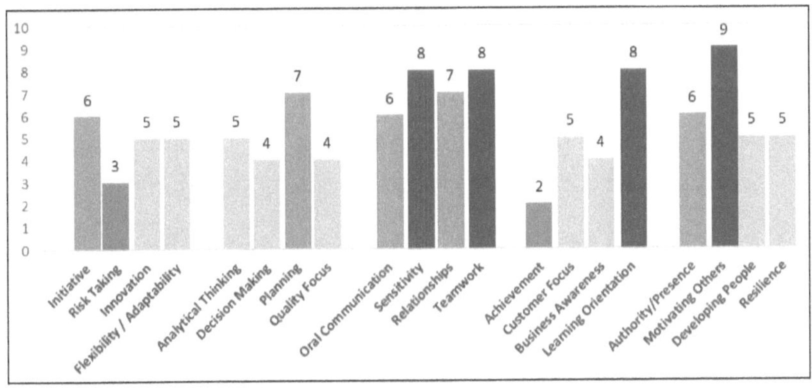

Figure 4: Representing the PPC 20 scores of Mr. X

1–3 being Low, 4 & 5 being Moderate, 6 & 7 being Good and 8–10 being Over Strength. Scores of 6 and 7 are considered ideal and people would deliver best when their scores on competencies fall in this range.

Low and Over Strength scores have its own positive and negative implications. **Over strength** scores should **not be looked as in gradation**, wherein high scores are interpreted to be excellent, as they would also carry its own negative implications.

All scores are always interpreted with respect to the current environmental situation in which the person is, as well as his/her work roles and responsibilities.

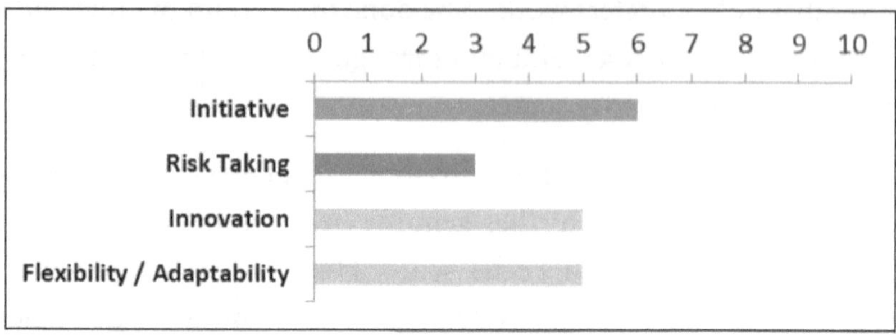

Figure 4.1: Representing the Scores of the competency – Managing Change of Mr. X

Managing Change Average score – 4.75

- **Initiative (6 – Good score)** refers to the ability to **begin an activity, task or managerial action**; be proactive and in control of what happens. The score indicates the subject takes responsibility and completes the assigned work, prefers to get a head start on the work at hand, tends to be hands-on, does not hesitate to begin working and confidently approaches new situations.

- **Risk Taking (3 – Low score)** refers to the **ability to take risks, to make things better and have courage to challenge rules and procedures.** The score shows that the subject takes cautious steps to obtain assured results, tends to avoid dealing with risky situations, comes across as a safe pair of hands who minimizes risks, works within the zone of familiarity, follows rules and procedures stringently and may resist new opportunities and paths.

- **Innovation (5 – Moderate score)** refers to the ability to **generate ideas and put them into practice**. The score expresses that the subject seeks variety within comfort zone, may rely on others to come up with innovative ideas, strives to bring in continuous improvement within existing systems and is open to incremental changes as long as it is backed by sufficient evidence of success.

- **Flexibility/Adaptability (5 – Moderate score)** refers to the ability to **respond flexibly to people/situations and being open**

and adaptable. The score indicates that the subject is capable of adapting to new techniques and methods with appropriate support, is willing to make compromises for others to maintain harmony. He/she might find it difficult to adjust quickly to abrupt/unexpected changes.

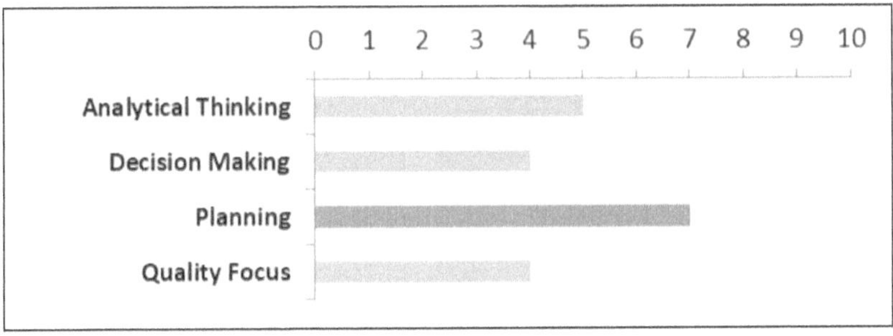

Figure 4.2: Representing the Scores of the competency – Planning &
Organising of Mr. X

Planning & Organizing Average score – 5

- **Analytical Thinking (5 – Moderate score)** refers to the **ability to think scientifically, logically and systematically.** The scores exhibit that the subject conducts analysis but **can also think on one's feet** when necessary, breaks problems down into key issues, quickly analyses various angles to arrive at judgements, considers the relevant facts before forming conclusions and may rely on instincts when pressed for time.

- **Decision Making (4 – Moderate score)** refers to the ability to **make quick, sound and effective decisions.** The scores show that the subject is capable of taking quick decisions when there is clarity of outcomes and takes decisions that do not upset the existing balance. When unsure, he/she may take decisions with the support of authority figures and can take simple decisions that are not crucial to critical business outcomes.

- **Planning (7 – Good score)** refers to the ability to **plan and organize resources.** The score suggests that the subject makes detailed plans to promote efficient functioning, prioritizes activities to meet set timelines, prefers to be well prepared and does groundwork before beginning any task, is likely to fall back on plans and follow the same carefully to deliver accurate results and comes across as a well-organized person.

- **Quality Focus (4 – Moderate score)** refers to the ability to **pay attention to details, meeting quality standards and deadlines.** This implies the subject delves into relevant details while keeping broad goals in sight, strives to deliver according to set standards of quality when there is sufficient time and less pressure, but may decrease the overall quality by compromising on either the pace of delivery or accuracy of work.

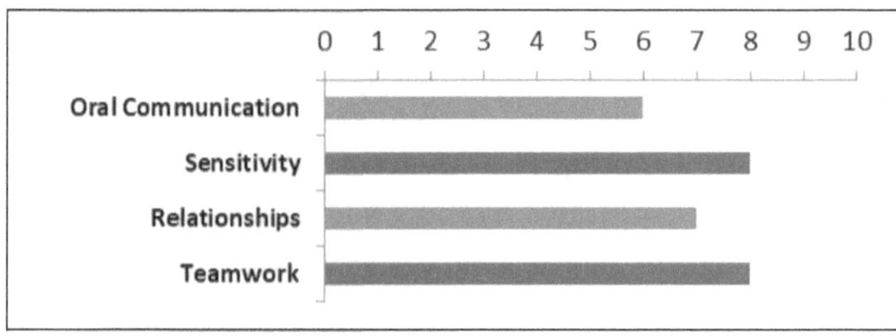

Figure 4.3: Representing the Scores of the competency – Interpersonal Skills of Mr. X

Interpersonal Skills Total Score – 7.25

- **Oral Communication (6 – Good score)** refers to the ability to **persuade and influence through communication.** The subject's score denotes that he/she can confidently initiate conversations and discussions, articulate, expresses thoughts with clarity, engages others and makes impactful presentations to gain others' buy-in.

- **Sensitivity (8 – Over strength score)** refers to the ability to **respond sensitively to others' needs and having positive regard**

for others. The score indicates that the subject listens carefully to others and is highly responsive to their problems, may tolerate poor performance and find it highly challenging to take decisions that may adversely affect others, compromising business goals to address others' problems.

- **Relationships (7 – Good score)** refers to the **ability to build rapport and get along easily with others**. The score implies that the subject enjoys people contact and wants to be surrounded by people, tends to be outgoing, friendly and enthusiastic in interactions, relates well with people and initiates conversations, is able to establish rapport and maintains a wide network of associations.

- **Teamwork (8 – Over strength score)** refers to the **ability to work effectively in teams**. The score suggests that the subject is highly collaborative and team-oriented in nature, finds it difficult to work without people interaction, requires others' support to deliver quality results and wants to avoid confrontations and may contribute greatly to groupthink.

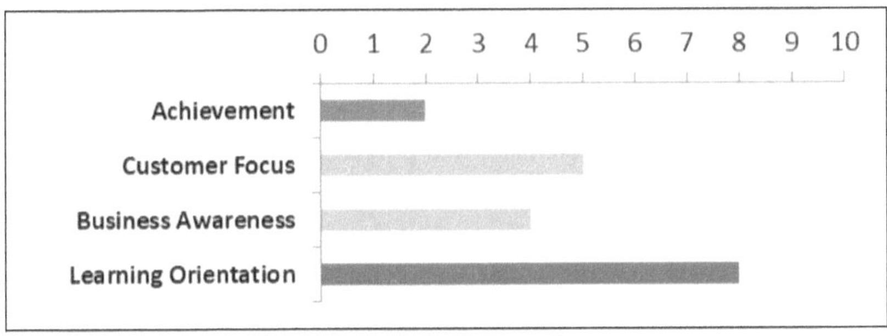

Figure 4.4: Representing the Scores of the competency – Result Orientation of Mr. X

Result Orientation Total Score – 4.75

- **Achievement (2 – Low score)** refers to the drive to **achieve results and experience success**. The score indicates, the subject is content with current position, is not highly competitive, puts personal life and family obligations first, comes across as lacking in drive, may not display initiative to meet targets and may not be able to "win" at business.

- **Customer Focus (5 – Moderate score)** refers to the **commitment to customer service, customer relations and customer benefits.** The score exhibits the subject's tendency to be courteous and well-mannered with customers, listen to client's complaints and improve services when issues are brought to notice, and maintain cordial interactions with both internal and external customers.

- **Business Awareness (4 – Moderate score)** refers to the **awareness of the profession, industry and competition.** The score expresses that the subject finds opportunities to enhance team's productivity, strives to utilize resources optimally, tends to monitor expenditures, is aware of one's area of expertise and keeps abreast with recent changes in the market.

- **Learning Orientation (8 – Over strength score)** refers to the commitment to **improve self through learning; the key to acquire all other competencies.** The score implies that the subject is eager to create and capitalize on every opportunity for development, displays a passion for continuous improvement, strives to optimize one's potential to the fullest, but may come across as a passenger and may compromise business performance at times.

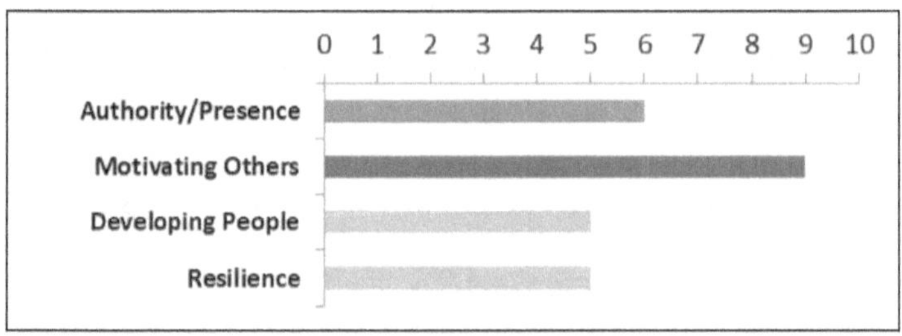

Figure 4.5: Representing the Scores of the competency –Leadership of Mr. X

Leadership Total Score – 6.25

- **Authority/Presence (6 – Good score)** refers to the ability to make **one's presence felt by exhibiting confidence**. The subject's score suggests that the subject projects an aura of self-confidence and carries oneself well, influences others through charismatic presence, is able to wield influence and tends to motivate and inspire others to accomplish the goal at hand.

- **Motivating Others (9 – Over strength score)** refers to the ability to **manage a team through delegation and empowerment.** As indicated by the scores, the subject inspires others to tap into the team's abilities and motivate them to achieve results. He/she may place too much faith in the potential of the team even though they may not deliver required outcomes, thereby coming across as too trusting.

- **Developing People (5 – Moderate score)** refers to the ability to **help members of the team diagnose and develop their skills**. As suggested by the score, the subject may provide others with opportunities to realize their own potential, acts as a role model for others to follow, is attentive towards the growth of team members, helps others learn from their mistakes when asked to share feedback and may take time out to teach others, should the need arise.

- **Resilience (5 – Moderate score)** indicates **physical and mental toughness and self-control**. The subject's score implies that the subject can perform when under pressure with adequate support, may cope with difficult situations to an extent, can handle a certain amount of stress in familiar situations, may be confident to handle challenges within area of specialization but can lose control if situations go spiralling out of hands and takes time to bounce back from failures.

BAT 3 Discussion: FITS, 4C's and PPC20

Feeler	Intuitor	Thinker	Sensor
28.5	23	21.5	27
Controlling (C1)	**Convincing (C2)**	**Conforming (C3)**	**Consistent (C4)**
27	22	27	24
Active Initiator (C1+C2)	**Passive Responder (C3+C4)**	**Task Oriented (C1+C3)**	**People Oriented (C2+C4)**
49	51	54	46

Performance Competency	Dimensions	Scores	Average
Managing Change	Initiative	6	4.75
	Risk Taking	3	
	Innovation	5	
	Flexibility/Adaptability	5	
Planning & Organising	Analytical Thinking	5	5
	Decision Making	4	
	Planning	7	
	Quality Forces	4	
Interpersonal Skills	Oral Communication	6	7.25
	Sensitivity	8	
	Relationships	7	
	Teamwork	8	
Result Orientation	Achievement	2	4.75
	Customer Focus	5	
	Business Awareness	4	
	Learning Orientation	8	
Leadership	Authority/Presence	6	6.25
	Motivating Others	9	
	Developing People	5	
	Resilience	5	

Through the FITS scores it can be interpreted that this individual is a **primary Feeler**. This indicates that he/she is inherently driven by emotions and has the potential to pick up on emotional cues and respond in a sensitive manner. Similarly, as interpreted through the PPC20 **Sensitivity score**, he/she is very sensitive to people's needs and feelings and is likely to listen to others and pay attention to their concerns, coming across as **considerate and caring**. His/her Teamwork score indicates that he/she is considered a **strong team player** and is perceived to be very helpful and supportive. This aligns well with the **Feeler and Sensor scores**, as they are likely to be people who require him/her to work, enjoy **people interaction** and are also **result focused**, the combination of which indicates a preference towards **achieving results through collaboration**.

The subject is also goal driven by nature and has an action-oriented approach to tasks. The Controlling score, indicating that he/she is **willing to tackle challenges confidently** to overcome barriers and persevere, also corroborate his/her sensor score. But on contrary through his/her PPC20 scores it can be interpreted that he/she is **not highly Task** and **Result oriented**, as the subject has scored **low on Achievement**. Thus, this **opposes the interpretation of the FITS and 4Cs score.** He/she also has the ability to approach a situation from multiple angles and generate different methods of completing tasks when the situation demands. However, as indicated by the high Conforming scores, the individual is unlikely to do this, preferring to **stick to the established routines** as it provides a **sense of security**. This is also backed by his/her **low risk-taking score** in PPC20 making him/her **resist change** when the situation is ambiguous to further reduce risks.

Though his/her Thinker score is the lowest, he/she has developed the ability to work in a structured and organized manner, delve into details and ensure accuracy. This is evidently learned behaviour as the innate potential to do so is low. His/her PPC20 score of **Planning** and **Analytical Thinking** also indicates that he/she is competent to make logical and rational decisions and will get into details with systematic approach, throwing light on the idea that current environment has helped in the reinforcement of these competencies which is opposing the inherent behaviour.

Moreover, while he/she is primarily a Feeler, his/her people orientation is uncharacteristically low, but PPC20 interprets him/her to be **good** in his/her **interpersonal skills** with having over strength in Sensitivity and Teamwork and having good scores in Oral Communications and Relationships. This indicates environmental influences and current requirements rendered him/her to adopt behaviours contradictory to his/her inherent nature in order to adapt. These aforementioned inferences were drawn as a result of linking the scores of the three assessments, as the three in isolation mention contradictory traits.

BAT 4 Discussion: FITS, 4C's, CPA and PPC20

Feeler	Intuitor	Thinker	Sensor
28.5	23	21.5	27
Controlling (C1)	**Convincing (C2)**	**Conforming (C3)**	**Consistent (C4)**
27	22	27	24
Active Initiator (C1+C2)	**Passive Responder (C3+C4)**	**Task Oriented (C1+C3)**	**People Oriented (C2+C4)**
49	51	54	46
Advise	**Criticize**	**Empathy**	**Search**
18	2	10	15

Performance Competency	Dimensions	Scores	Average
Managing Change	Initiative	6	4.75
	Risk Taking	3	
	Innovation	5	
	Flexibility/Adaptability	5	
Planning & Organising	Analytical Thinking	5	5
	Decision Making	4	
	Planning	7	
	Quality Focus	4	
Interpersonal Skills	Oral Communication	6	7.25
	Sensitivity	8	
	Relationships	7	
	Teamwork	8	

Result Orientation	Achievement	2	4.75
	Customer Focus	5	
	Business Awareness	4	
	Learning Orientation	8	
Leadership	Authority/Presence	6	6.25
	Motivating Others	9	
	Developing People	5	
	Resilience	5	

Through the FITS scores it can be interpreted that the subject is a **primary Feeler**. This indicates that the subject is **inherently driven by emotions** and has the potential to pick up on emotional cues and respond in a **sensitive** manner. Similarly, as interpreted through the PPC20 Sensitivity score, the subject is very sensitive to people's needs and feelings and is likely to **listen to others** and pay attention to their concerns, coming across as **considerate** and **caring**. Through the subject's CPA score it can be interpreted that Advise score is high, and Empathy is low suggesting that the subject is most likely to **give recommendations** and suggestions during communication rather than getting to **know the perspective** of the individual being communicated to.

This interpretation also explains the subject's low score of People Orientation in 4cs. The subject's **Teamwork** score indicates that he/she is considered a **strong team player** and is perceived to be very helpful and supportive. This aligns well with the Feeler and Sensor scores, as they are likely to be people who want to work, enjoy people interaction and are also result focused, the combination of which indicates a preference towards achieving results through collaboration. As the subject's **Advise** score is dominant, it can be interpreted that he/she is most likely to give guidance to his/her team members.

With **Learning Orientation** being an over strength as interpreted through the PPC20 score, the subject is likely to create and capitalize on every opportunity for development and approach learning enthusiastically. Thus, displaying a **passion for continuous improvement**, striving to optimize one's potential to the fullest. He/she is highly interested in a variety of topics and concepts. Thus, being congruent with his/her **Sensor** and **Intuito**r scores in FITS.

With the primary scores on 4Cs being both **Controlling** and **Conforming**, the subject is likely to accept challenges and take charge of the situations but will implement changes that **bring about improvements in the existing system**. He/she might not do well in tackling new difficulties requiring him/her to deviate from the prescribed standards. This also corroborates with the subject's moderate score on **Resilience** in PPC20.

The subject is also goal driven by nature and has an action-oriented approach to tasks. The **Controlling** score in 4c, indicating that he/she is willing to tackle challenges confidently to overcome barriers and persevere, also corroborate with his/her Sensor score. But on the **contrary,** he/she may not take up initiative to meet targets and may not be highly competitive or ambitious as interpreted through his/her low score on **Achievement** in PPC20, Thus, this opposes the interpretation of the FITS and 4Cs score.

With a primary **Conforming** score and moderate Decision-Making scores, he/she is capable of taking decisions but will make sure that it is **accepted by others** and is **aligned with the standards prescribed**. With high motivation score in PPC20, he/she will also encourage others to get on board with his/her decisions. This may cause delay in the decision-making process. The subject has a low score of **Criticize** in CPA which validates the subjects over strength in motivation as he/she is most likely to avoid denouncing anyone and will **focus more on encouraging others for development**.

The subject has a good **Search** score in CPA suggesting that he/she is most likely to probe and inquire which helps in him/her approach a situation from multiple angles and generate different methods of completing tasks when the situation demands. However, as indicated by the high **Conforming** scores, the individual is unlikely to do this, **preferring to stick to the established standards as it provides a sense of security**. This is also backed by the subject's low **Risk-Taking** score in PPC20 making him/her resist change when the situation is ambiguous, to further reduce risks.

Though the subject's **Thinker** score is the lowest, the subject has developed the **ability to work in a structured and organized manner, delve into details** and **ensure accuracy**. This is evidently learned behaviour as the innate potential to do so is low. The subject's PPC20 score on **Planning** and **Analytical Thinking** also indicates that the subject is competent to make **logical and rational decisions** and is likely to proceed with tasks in a **systematic manner**, throwing light on the aspect that the **current environment** has helped in the **reinforcement of these competencies** which is **opposing the inherent behaviour**.

Moreover, although the subject is a primary Feeler, his/her people orientation is uncharacteristically low. On the contrary, PPC20 interprets him/her to be good in his/her Interpersonal Skills, while having an over strength in **Sensitivity** and **Teamwork** and having good scores in **Oral Communication** and **Relationships**. This indicates environmental influences and current requirements rendered him/her to adopt behaviours contradictory to the subject's inherent nature in order to adapt. These aforementioned inferences were drawn as a result of linking the scores of the four assessments, as the four in isolation mention contradictory traits.

5. BPA

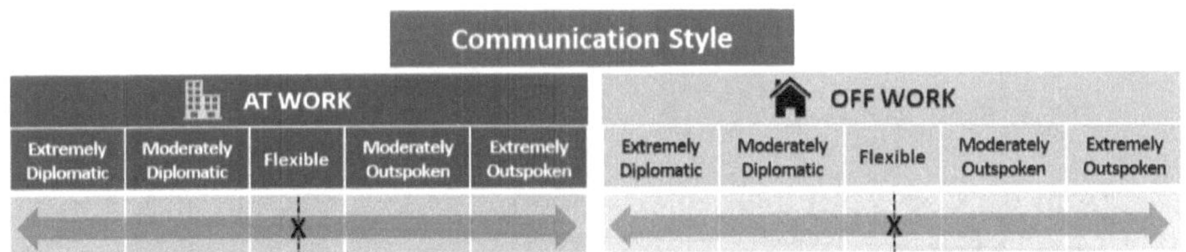

Figure 5.1: Representing the Scores of the Communication style of Mr. X at work and off work

From the above pictorial representation, it is seen that the subject seems to be **flexible in his/her Communication Style both at and off work**. Based on the situation, the subject tends to adopt either an outspoken or tactful approach while communicating. He/she can communicate in a self-assured and straightforward manner and is likely to state thoughts in a diplomatic way when required. He/she is inclined to resolve conflicts through negotiation and open discussions and strikes a balance between giving instructions and making requests when getting things done.

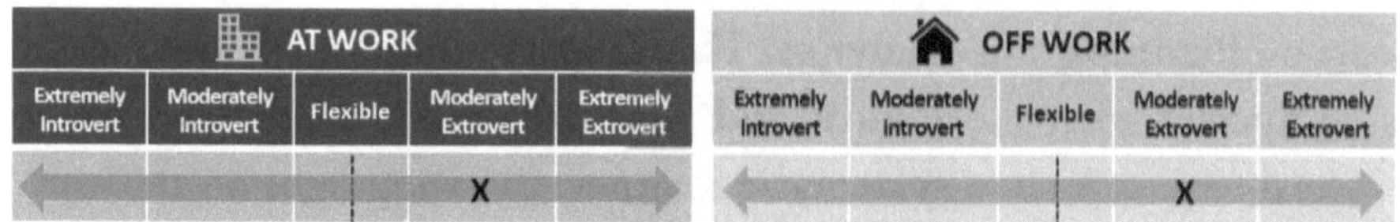

Figure 5.2: Representing the Interpersonal Relations Scores of Mr. X at work and off work

From the above pictorial representation, it is seen that the subject seems to be **Moderately Extrovert in his/her way of interacting with people both at and off work**. The subject enjoys people-contact and is able to establish rapport easily, maintaining a large network of associations. He/she is able to relate well with people and get along well in team-settings. The subject is likely to be energized by social activities and events and lack of people contact and group support is likely to be stressful for him/her.

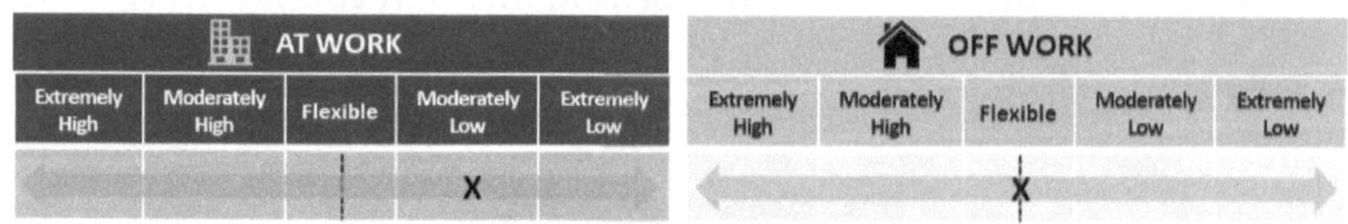

Figure 5.3: Representing Sense of Urgency Scores of Mr. X at work and off work

From the above pictorial representation, it is seen that the subject seems to have a **Moderately Low Sense of Urgency at work and is flexible at and off work**. The subject enjoys working on long-term projects that require calculated responses and considers various options when making a choice, taking the time to analyse them. He/she likes to adopt a consistent and stable approach while completing activities, gets things done through perseverance and persistence. Frequent interruptions are likely to cause him/her stress and may in turn cause delays and they may find short deadlines and high-pressure situations to be stressful.

In domestic situations, the subject can flex between high and low sense of urgency depending on the situation and can manage multiple responsibilities when required. Also, he/she may take on a steadier and relaxed approach, if time allows and typically considers a range of options before making a choice.

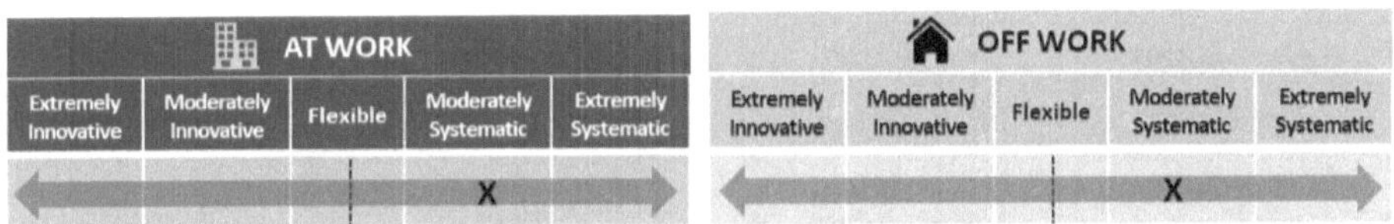

Figure 5.4: Representing Information Processing Scores of Mr. X at work and off work

From the above pictorial representation, it is seen that the subject seems to have a **moderately systematic approach in Processing Information** both **at and off work**. The subject tends to organize activities and proceeds with work only after conducting thorough research about the aspects he/she would be dealing with. He/she delves into details in a systematic manner to ensure accuracy and prepares to-do lists and plans to enhance his/her efficiency. The subject may become frustrated by ambiguity and lack of specific guidelines for tasks and may respond to such stress by getting further into minute details.

BAT 5 Discussion: FITS, 4C's, CPA, BPA and PPC20

Feeler	Intuitor	Thinker	Sensor
28.5	23	21.5	27
Controlling (C1)	**Convincing (C2)**	**Conforming (C3)**	**Consistent (C4)**
27	22	27	24
Active initiator C1 + C2)	**Passive responder (C3 + C4)**	**Task oriented (C1 + C3)**	**People oriented (C2 + C4)**
49	51	54	46

Advise	Criticize	Empathy	Search
18	2	10	15
Parameter	**Dimensions**	**At Work**	**Off work**
Communication Style	Diplomatic/ Outspoken	Flexible	Flexible
Interpersonal Relations	Extrovert/Introvert	Moderately Extrovert	Moderately Extrovert
Sense of Urgency	High/Low	Moderately Low	Flexible
Information Processing	Systematic/ Innovative	Moderately Systematic	Moderately Systematic
Performance Competency	**Dimensions**	**Scores**	**Average**
Managing Change	Initiative	6	4.75
	Risk Taking	3	
	Innovation	5	
	Flexibility/ Adaptability	5	
Planning & Organising	Analytical Thinking	5	5
	Decision Making	4	
	Planning	7	
	Quality Focus	4	
Interpersonal Skills	Oral Communication	6	7.25
	Sensitivity	8	
	Relationships	7	
	Teamwork	8	

Result Orientation	Achievement	2	4.75
	Customer Focus	5	
	Business Awareness	4	
	Learning Orientation	8	
Leadership	Authority/Presence	6	6.25
	Motivating Others	9	
	Developing People	5	
	Resilience	5	

The subject's **Feeler** score indicates that he/she is likely to be warm and friendly, coming across as approachable. He/she is concerned about people's moods/feelings and is typically sensitive to others' emotions. He/she has the ability to build relationships easily and get along with others. Having a **Relationship** score of 7, the subject relates well with people and initiates conversations, is able to establish rapport and maintains a wide network of associations that could double as resources. The subject is also moderately an **Extrovert** at work and off work, which indicates that he/she can express his/her feelings readily in open manner and prefers to interact with lot of people and enjoys interacting with others. Having a **Sensitivity** score of 8 which is an over strength implies the subject would respond to people in a helpful manner, which can be corroborated by his/her **Advise** score, indicating his/her genuine desire to help others. The subject's **Oral Communication** scores also indicate that he/she can confidently **initiate conversations** and discussions. He/she has the ability to express thoughts with clarity and conciseness.

His/her **Controlling** score also indicates that he/she prefers work to be done in a certain manner, aiming for precision and quality as exhibited through conforming scores. He/she is action oriented which means, the subject takes responsibility and completes the assigned work. Having a low **Risk-Taking** score, he/she is likely to align himself/herself to established policies, methodologies and procedures to avoid uncertainty and ensure predictability. This corroborates with his/her **Conforming** scores implying he/she may be wary of novelty and changes. Further, as **Flexibility** is moderate, the subject is likely to take time to adjust to changes, provided he/she is sure that the change is **necessary for improvement, beneficial** and will **yield accurate results**. Being moderately **Resilient**, he/she is able to maintain composure during stressful situations and **deal with setbacks with patience.**

The individual's **Sense of Urgency** is moderately low at work, which means that he/she considers many options and alternatives before deciding. This also corresponds with the individual's **Decision – Making** score which is moderate, therefore he/she tends to make decisions slowly and is seen as prudent and careful. This could also be because of his/her **Analytical Thinking** score, which is again moderate, the individual tends to analyse things carefully and think things through when the situation demands. He/she also evaluates and considers options carefully.

Having a good score on **Planning and Organizing**, the individual tends to prioritize work activities, tackle tasks systematically and organize time effectively. This score correlates with **Information Processing** where the individual is moderately systematic, which indicates that he/she tends to organize details in a timely and thorough manner. He/she also uses established procedures to accomplish tasks. However, his/her **Quality Focus** scores in comparison are on the lower side, at a Moderate score of 4, indicating that while he/she is capable of identifying errors and making necessary corrections, the quality of work is not his/her primary focus. This is in contrast with his/her conforming scores but can be explained through his/her **Achievement** scores, which is low, indicating contentment about the current state of affairs.

Individual's score on **Teamwork** is 8 which implies an over strength – this means, the subject is highly collaborative and team-oriented in nature and may rely on his team to achieve the end goals. He/she may also find it difficult to work without people interaction, requiring others' support to deliver quality results. In his/her attempts to achieve objectives in collaboration, he/she is likely to strive to maintain the group cohesiveness. This would help him/her avoid friction in the team which would affect the facilitation of goal-attainment. This correlates with his/her feeler and consistent scores. As indicated by the moderate **Developing People** score, he/she may also provide others with opportunities to realize their own potential and is likely to be attentive towards the growth of team members. It could be quite possibly from a task focused point of view, to ensure that the group has the skills to undertake the complexities of the tasks.

Having a **Sensor** score of 27, the individual tends to be action oriented, and can make the most out of every opportunity. Being **Task Oriented**, he/she tends to give importance to task completion. When dealing with customers, he/she would listen to their concerns to the extent to gauge their requirements, as indicated by his **Customer Focus** and **Sensitivity** scores. Once he/she has understood their needs, he/she would proceed to suggest solutions or suggestions about how he/she intends to cater to the customer, as indicated by the **Advise** score. He/she may not try to understand the perspective of the client in terms of why the client desires what he/she desires and such, as exhibited by the **Empathy** score.

Similarly, when he/she is approached with issues or problems, he/she asks for additional information to get to the **root of the problem**. Once he/she has understood the task related aspects, he/she proceeds to provide solutions, not paying attention to the individual perspectives of the people involved. His/her **Advise** score, shows that he/she may proceed to recommend solutions to others out of his/her genuine desire to help, which is in alignment with the high Feeler score. In relation to his/her **Conforming and Controlling** scores, striving to ensure that things are done the "right" way, he/she resorts to providing detailed guidelines and suggestions on how to proceed with tasks.

The subject's **Learning Orientation** score is 8, implying an over strength, he/she displays a passion for continuous improvement and seems to have interests in a variety of topics. He/she is likely to be open to acquiring additional information about his/her field of work, thereby gaining knowledge and expertise. His/her moderate **Business Awareness** scores implies that he/she is aware and keeps abreast with the recent developments in their industry. This inference is in tandem with the **Learning Orientation** scores, indicating that the subject tends to be aware of his/her methodologies in terms of implementing strategies into his/her work. In addition, his/her industry knowledge aids him/her in providing insightful insights to the team, thereby guiding them in all their professional endeavours.

6. VAK – Visual, Auditory and Kinesthetic learning styles

VAK assesses the various modes by which individuals prefer to acquire information based on their heredity characteristics.

Table 6: Representing the VAK Scores of Mr. X

Visual	Auditory	Kinesthetic
33	31	36

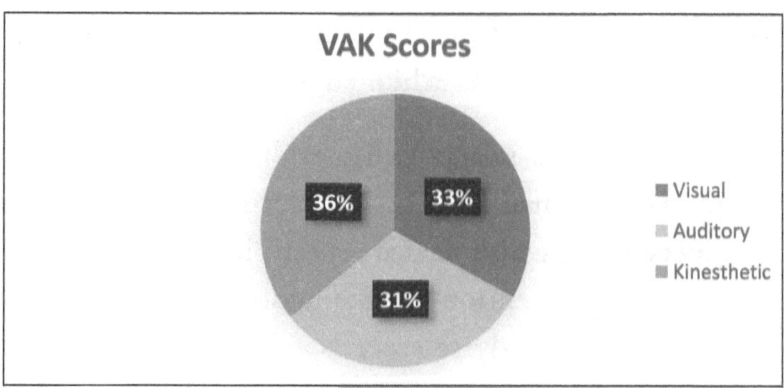

Figure 6: Representing the VAK Scores of Mr. X

From table 6, it is evident that the subject has scored 33, 31 and 36 in the Visual, Auditory and the Kinesthetic dimensions of learning styles respectively, the highest being for the Kinesthetic Learning Styles.

Referring to Figure 6, it is evident that the subject has a primary score (36%) in the Kinesthetic learning style dimension and the secondary score (33%) pertaining to Visual learning style.

Preferring to be **directly involved in the learning experience**, the subject enjoys athletics, gaming, sculpting and such. The subject may find it **hard to sit still for long periods** and may become distracted by their need for activity and exploration. Thus, preferring to learn through **hands-on experiences**, he/she tends to **lose concentration** if there is **little or no external stimulation or movement**.

Visual learning style being the subject's second dominant learning style; he/she tends to **retain information through reading** or **seeing**. The subject may **think in terms of pictures** or **written instructions** and **learn best** from **visual displays** including: diagrams, illustrated text books, overhead transparencies, videos, flipcharts and hand-outs.

Auditory learning style being the subject's other strength as well, he/she would also be comfortable **gaining** and **retaining information** by **listening** to someone. He/she may be seen with a group of people being **involved in lengthy discussions**.

7. PRSE – Learning Style Preferences

Table 7: Representing the PRSE Scores of Mr. X

Learning Style	Participative	Reflective	Experimental	Structured
Scores	26	25.5	26	22.5

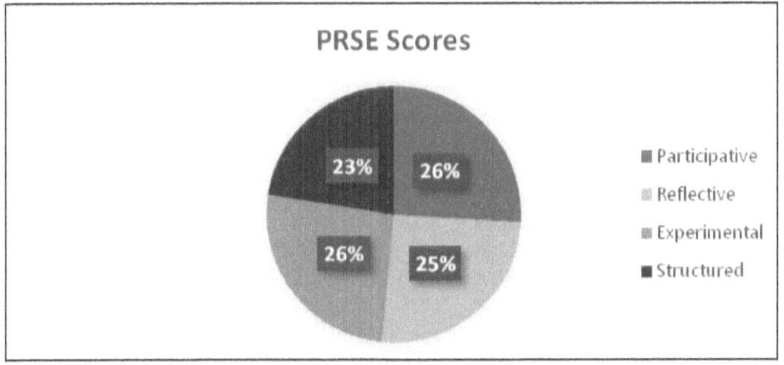

Figure 7: Representing the PRSE Scores of Mr. X

From table 7, it is evident that the subject has scored 26, 25.5, 26 and 22.5 in the Participative, Reflective, Experimental and the Structured dimensions of learning style preferences respectively.

Referring to Figure 7, it is evident that the subject has a primary score (26%) in the Participative and Experiential learning style dimension and also in the Structured learning style dimensions with 25% of the score.

With relatively equal scores across all four learning style preferences, based on the demands of the learning environment, the subject may be able to cope with ease. He/she tends to place importance on understanding as well as on practical application.

Being a **Participative learner**, the subject may come across as an **extrovert**, who is sociable and outgoing, enjoying collaborative activities. He/she may tend to be **open to new experiences** and this may serve as a **motivator for him/her to learn new things**. He/she would like to be personally involved in a learning event, as it may help him/her understand things better.

The subject's score on **Experimental style** of learning suggests that he/she is motivated to try things out and see how it works. Having **practical orientation**, he/she tends to look for **clear application with focus** on what works. This may give him/her a **hands-on understanding** of why things happen the way they do.

The subject's moderate score on **Reflective learning style** indicates that he/she has the **ability to accumulate information** from various sources to attain a **well-rounded understanding**. He/she may reflect on their own or with others, seeking various opinions before reaching a decision. The subject's **inquisitive nature** and **keen observation skills** guide him/her to be adept at perceiving and understanding diverse information and experiences.

With the lowest score obtained by the subject being Structured learning, while he/she may benefit from sequential and delineated lessons, he/she **would also be comfortable dealing with ambiguity**. The subject may not follow systematic way of doing things and may not enjoy quantitative analysis, as it does not come naturally to him/her.

8. **CARS – Concrete, Abstract, Random and Sequential Learning Style Stages**

CARS assess the stages in which an individual prefers to assimilate information based on four classifications (Concrete Sequential, Abstract Sequential, Concrete Random and Abstract Random). The individual's scores provide an objective tool to understand the means by which he/she acquires new learning.

Table 8: Representing the CARS Scores of Mr. X

Learning Style	Abstract Random	Concrete Random	Concrete Sequential	Abstract Sequential
Scores	31	29	19	21

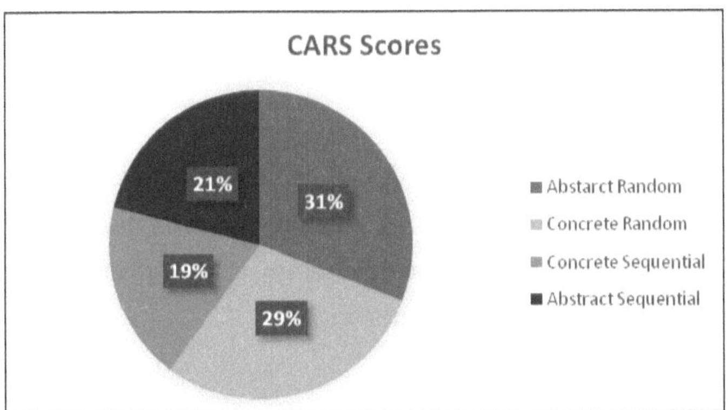

Figure 8: Representing the CARS Scores of Mr. X

From table 8, it is evident that the subject has scored 31, 29, 19 and 21 in the Abstract Random, Concrete Random, Concrete Sequential and the Abstract Sequential Learning Style respectively. Referring to Figure 8, it is evident that the subject has a primary score (31%) in the Abstract Random dimension and the secondary score (29%) belonging to the Concrete Sequential Learning Style.

With **high score** on **Abstract Random** learning style, the subject tends to **make use of imagination** as a ready resource to experience learning. He/she enjoys doing projects/assignments that require **personalization**. As someone who enjoys group activities, the subject is likely to listen to others and consider their inputs.

The subject's score on **Concrete Random** learning style suggests that he/she is likely to **try new approaches of solving problems**. Being self-directed, he/she tends to experiment to find answers using **trial and error method** and is willing to take risks. The subject enjoys challenging environment and tends to compete with others. It may be a challenge for the subject to work when there are stringent restrictions and limitations. The subject **may not enjoy keeping detailed records**.

The subject's **low score on Abstract Sequential** learning style suggests that he/she is likely to go with the flow, thereby **not being inclined towards analysis and in-depth examination** before deciding or acting. While the subject can deal with theory and concepts that delve into cause-effect relationships, he/she is likely to retain more when learning involves active participation.

Having preference for innovation, as indicated by his/her **low Concrete Sequential** method, he/she is **not drawn towards facts and concrete information**. Thus, in order to bring changes and improve systems, he/she may prefer new/better ways of doing things.

9. **Multiple Intelligence (MI):**

Table 9: Representing the MI Scores of Mr. X

Multiple Intelligence	Score
Linguistic	17
Logical	16
Rhythmic	19
Visual	17
Kinesthetic	17
Inter-Personal	20

Intra-Personal	19
Naturalistic	17
Meta-Physical	18

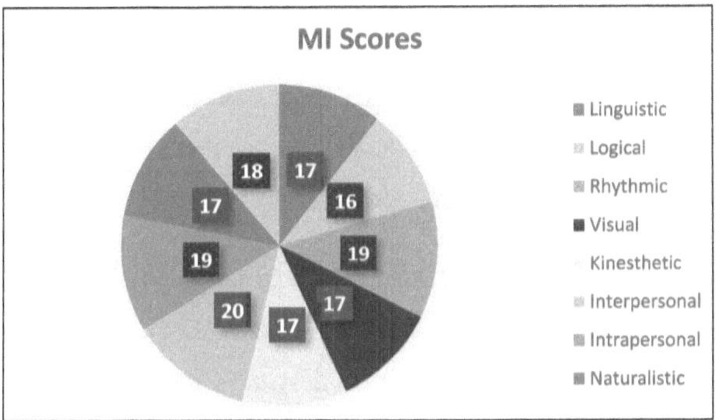

Figure 10.2: Representing the MI Scores of Mr. X

With the range of scores and their interpretations being 6–12 yet to be nurtured, 13–18 fairly developed and 19–24 strongly developed, it can be said that the subject's Rhythmic, Interpersonal and Intrapersonal Intelligences are strongly developed, and the remaining are fairly developed.

With high **Interpersonal Intelligence**, the subject's strength lies in **interacting with people** and **understanding/being sensitive** towards their state of mind. The subject is adept at **expressing** his/her **thoughts and feelings** in an **open manner** with his/her loved ones.

The subject's **Intrapersonal Intelligence** score implies that he/she is likely to be **aware** of his/her **emotional state** and **motivations**. He/she may tend to take time out to **introspect**.

The subject's score on **Rhythmic/Musical Intelligence** indicates that he/she has an **ear for rhythm** and **enjoys different genres of music**. He/she is sensitive to pitch, timbre, rhythm and tones of the music. **Listening to music,** singing or playing an instrument could be his/her **favourite pastime.** The subject may learn better when he/she has soothing music/favourite music playing in the back ground. Thus, music can support him/her in their learning process.

With fairly developed **Spiritual/Metaphysical Intelligence**, the subject is likely to **engage** in **activities** that develop his/her **spiritual well-being** and in turn makes a difference in the way he/she lives. The subject thoroughly **likes** and **enjoys thinking, questioning**, and may be **curious** about **life, death & ultimate realities**.

The subject has the ability to **express** and **appreciate complex meanings**. The subject displays an ability to **persuade others** and draws people towards self through **articulation**.

The score on **Visual/Spatial Intelligence** implies that the subject has the ability to **manipulate and create mental images** easily. With a tendency to daydream, the subject displays capability to imagine and makes sense of concepts that are not necessarily tangible. With his/her pretty good sense of direction, he/she may be good at finding his/her way around new places.

The subject's score on **Kinesthetic Intelligence** indicates that he/she is comfortable being **physically active**. The subject likes to engage self in **outdoor activities** like taking up field work, indulging in sports, shopping, going for walks etc. The subject may **learn best by hands-on experiences, role-plays or drama**.

With the subject's **Naturalistic Intelligence**, he/she is interested to **understand** and be **involved** with **nature**. He/she may **learn best** by **working in nature**, exploring living things, learning about plants and natural events. He/she may **enjoy outdoor activities like gardening, hiking, camping** etc.

The subject may **think conceptually, abstractly** and has the **capacity to discern patterns** and **relationships**. He/she tends to be **curious about the world around** and **ask lots of questions** and likes to **get involved in activities** that includes grouping, categorizing, recognizing relationships, creating order out of chaos, predicting etc.

BAT 6 Discussion: FITS, 4C's, VAK, CARS, PRSE, MI

Feeler	Intuitor	Thinker	Sensor
28.5	23	21.5	27
Controlling (C1)	Convincing (C2)	Conforming (C3)	Consistent (C4)
27	22	27	24
Active Initiator (C1+C2)	Passive Responder (C3+C4)	Task Oriented (C1+C3)	People Oriented (C2+C4)
49	51	54	46

Visual	Auditory	Kinesthetic
33	31	36

Learning Style	Abstract Random	Concrete Random	Concrete Sequential	Abstract Sequential
Scores	31	29	19	21
Learning Style	Participative	Reflective	Experimental	Structured
Scores	26	25.5	26	22.5

Multiple Intelligence	Score
Linguistic	17
Logical	16
Rhythmic	19
Visual	17
Kinesthetic	17
Inter-personal	20
Intra-personal	19
Naturalistic	17
Meta-physical	18

As indicated by the FITS scores, the individual is a **primary Feeler, secondary Sensor, median Intuitor and low Thinker**. This indicates that he/she has the inherent potential to **pick up on emotional cues** and respond in a **sensitive** manner. The subject is also **goal driven** by nature and has an **action-oriented** approach to tasks. The Controlling score, indicating that he/she is willing to **deal with challenges confidently** to **overcome barriers**, also affirm his/her Sensor score. He/She displays the **determination** to carry on with a course of action even in the face of difficulty, as depicted by the Consistent scores. He/she also has the potential to approach a situation from multiple angles and generate different methods of completing tasks when the situation demands. However, as indicated by the high Conforming scores, the individual is unlikely to do this, preferring to abide by the **conventional methods** as it provides a **sense of security** and guarantees **predictability**.

Though his/her Thinker score is the lowest, he/she has developed the ability to work in a **structured and organized** manner, delve into details and ensure accuracy. This is in accordance with his/her Logical Intelligence score, which develops over time implying that this is evidently learned behaviour as the innate potential to do so is low. Moreover, although he/she is primarily a Feeler, his/her **People Orientation is uncharacteristically low**. This indicates **environmental influences** rendered him/her to adopt behaviours contradictory to his/her inherent nature in order to adapt. It also indicates that his/her true potentials were not allowed to develop by a thwarting environment.

The individual's scores on VAK indicate that while he/she primarily prefers the **Kinesthetic** mode of learning, he/she can also incorporate information when it is presented in the Visual and Auditory modes respectively. He/she tends to learn best when **directly involved in the learning experience**, displaying a hands-on orientation. This is in congruence with his/her Sensor and Controlling scores, portraying the **need for action and results**. His/her Experimental, Concrete Random and Kinesthetic Intelligence scores are in tandem with his learning preference, indicating that the subject **understands concepts with clarity** when he/she can **apply his/her knowledge practically** and learn through a **trial and error** approach. The subject may find it hard to sit still for long periods and may become distracted by their need for activity and exploration. Thus, he/she is likely to lose concentration if there is little or no external stimulation or movement.

The subject's second dominant learning style is **Visual**, indicating that he/she may be fast at reading and good at working with **details**. This is in accordance with his Visual Intelligence scores as well which implies that the subject has the ability to manipulate and create mental images easily. Coming across as a visual person, the subject may **think in terms of pictures** or written instructions and **learn best from visual displays** including diagrams, illustrated text books, videos, and hand-outs.

Auditory learning style being the subject's other strength as well, he/she would also be comfortable gaining and **retaining information by listening** to someone. He/she may be seen with a group of people being involved in **lengthy discussions**. This aligns with his/her Participative and Abstract Random scores which signifies that the subject tends to learn through **participation and interaction** with others. This is also supported by his/her strongly developed Interpersonal Intelligence score which denotes that he/she is likely to enjoy social interactions, making every situation a learning experience. In tandem with his/her abstract random learning style, group discussions and reading aloud would also prove beneficial for an auditory learner.

The subject's scores on the Multiple Intelligence scale range from moderate to high, implying that he/she has fairly developed to strongly developed intelligence among the nine types as defined by Gardner. His/her score on Linguistic Intelligence implies that the subject has a good **grasp over language** and is likely to be **articulate** in his/her communication, both verbal and written. With a fairly developed Logical Intelligence, as contrary to his/her low Thinker score, it can be implied that the subject has **developed the ability to deal with numbers and data** and can create patterns between the same to draw inferences.

The subject's high Intrapersonal Intelligence score implies that he/she is likely to be **aware of his/her emotional state and motivations**. He/she may tend to take time out to **introspect**. This is in accordance with his/her score on the Reflective style of learning indicating that the subject **internalises information** better by using his/her **own imagination and thought to add meaning** to his/her learning and experiences.

The subject displays high scores in the aspects of Rhythmic, Naturalistic and Metaphysical Intelligence, signifying his/her **creative bent of mind** as denoted by a median Intuitor score. The subjects strongly developed Rhythmic Intelligence indicates that he/she has an ear for rhythm and enjoys different genres of music. His/her Naturalistic Intelligence score denotes his/her interest to understand and be involved with nature. He/she may learn best by **working in nature,** exploring living things, learning about plants and natural events. He/she may **enjoy outdoor activities** like gardening, hiking, camping etc. With a fairly developed Metaphysical Intelligence, the subject is likely to enjoy thinking, questioning and satiating his/her curiosity about life, death & ultimate realities.

BAT 4 Discussion: FITS, 4C's, MI and PPC20

Feeler	Intuitor	Thinker	Sensor
28.5	23	21.5	27
Controlling (C1)	**Convincing (C2)**	**Conforming (C3)**	**Consistent (C4)**
27	22	27	24
Active Initiator (C1+C2)	**Passive Responder (C3+C4)**	**Task Oriented (C1+C3)**	**People Oriented (C2+C4)**
49	51	54	46

Performance Competency	Dimensions	Scores	Average
Managing Change	Initiative	6	
	Risk Taking	3	
	Innovation	5	4.75
	Flexibility/ Adaptability	5	

Planning & Organising	Analytical Thinking	5	5
	Decision Making	4	
	Planning	7	
	Quality Focus	4	
Interpersonal Skills	Oral Communication	6	7.25
	Sensitivity	8	
	Relationships	7	
	Teamwork	8	
Result Orientation	Achievement	2	4.75
	Customer Focus	5	
	Business Awareness	4	
	Learning Orientation	8	
Leadership	Authority/Presence	6	6.25
	Motivating Others	9	
	Developing People	5	
	Resilience	5	

Multiple Intelligence	**Score**
Linguistic	17
Logical	16
Rhythmic	19
Visual	17
Kinesthetic	17
Inter-personal	20
Intra-personal	19
Naturalistic	17
Meta-physical	18

Through the FITS scores it can be understood that this individual is a primary Feeler. This indicates that he/she is inherently driven by emotions and has the potential to **pick up on emotional cues** and respond in a sensitive manner. High Feeler scores also indicates an **understanding**

of self, also determined by the Intrapersonal Intelligence, which in the subject's case in strongly developed, suggesting that he/she is likely to be **aware of his/her own emotions, moods, strengths, challenges and potentials**. His/her Interpersonal Intelligence is also strongly developed, thereby confirming the subject's **ability to build relationships**.

Similarly, as interpreted through the PPC20 Sensitivity score, he/she is very **sensitive to people's needs and feelings** and is likely to listen to others and pay attention to their concerns, coming across as **considerate and caring**. His/her Teamwork score indicates that he/she is considered a **strong team player** and is perceived to be very helpful and supportive. Thus, this aligns well with the Feeler and Sensor scores, as they are likely to be people who enjoy people interaction and are also result focused, the combination of which indicates a preference towards **achieving results through collaboration**. While his/her Convincing scores may be low, the fairly developed linguistic scores suggest that the subject is able to convey the thoughts and opinions effectively, and possibly in a straightforward manner that facilitates ease of understanding.

The subject is also **goal driven** by nature and has an **action-oriented** approach to tasks. The Sensor and Controlling score, indicating that he/she is willing to tackle challenges confidently to overcome barriers and persevere, also corroborate his/her sensor score. His/her Kinesthetic Intelligence also suggests that the subject is likely to enjoy a **hands-on approach** to tasks. But contrary to the subjects' high Task Oriented score, his/her PPC20 scores it can be interpreted that while he/she is **task and result oriented**, it is likely to be **regarding immediate targets** and not about goals for further development, as the subject has scored low on **Achievement.**

He/she also has the ability to approach a situation from multiple angles and generate different methods of completing tasks when the situation demands. However, as indicated by the high Conforming scores, the individual is unlikely to do this, preferring to stick to the **established routines** as it provides a **sense of security**. This is also backed by his/her low risk-taking score in PPC20 making him/her resist change when the situation is ambiguous to further reduce risks and is further supported by his/her fairly developed Logical Intelligence.

Though his/her **Thinker** score is the lowest, he/she has developed the ability to work in a **structured and organized manner**, delve into details and ensure accuracy. This is evidently learned behaviour as the innate potential to do so is low. His/her PPC20 score of **Planning** and **Analytical Thinking** also indicates that he/she is competent to make **logical and rational decisions** and will get into **details with systematic approach**, throwing light on the idea that current environment has helped in the reinforcement of these competencies which is opposing the inherent behaviour.

Moreover, he/she is primarily a Feeler, his/her **People Orientation** is uncharacteristically low, but PPC20 interprets him/her to be good in his/her **Interpersonal Skills** with having over strength in Sensitivity and Teamwork and having good scores in **Oral Communications** and **Relationships**. This indicates environmental influences and current requirements rendered him/her to adopt behaviours contradictory to his/her inherent nature in order to adapt.

Further, an interpretation of the remaining MI scores suggests that the subject has a strongly developed Visual Intelligence, suggesting that he/she can work well with visual stimuli. His/her **Rhythmic Intelligence** is also strongly developed. Parallels of these two aspects of intelligences can be drawn to match the median Intuitor score that suggests a moderately **creative bent of mind**. Similarly, the curious side of a median Intuitor is also apparent in the subject's fairly developed Naturalistic and Metaphysical intelligences, which indicates an inclination towards understanding the physical world and nature as well as abstract concepts such as mythology, spiritualism, cosmic realities and such.

These inferences were drawn as a result of linking the scores of the fours assessments, as the three in isolation mention contradictory traits.

10. **LEAP**

Table 10: Representing LEAP Scores of Mr. X

Director	Coach	Entrepreneur	Specialist
22	20	18	12

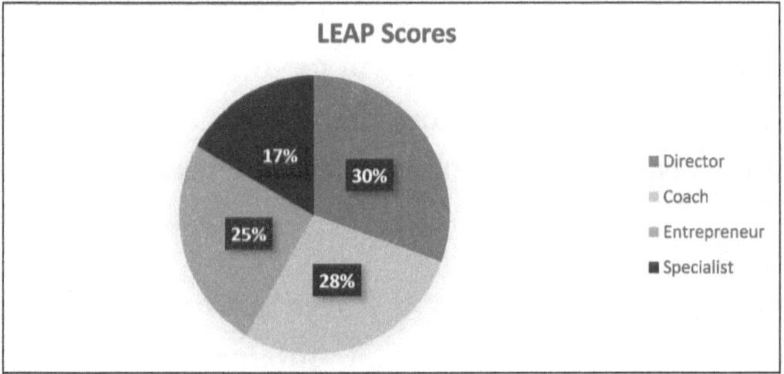

Figure 10: Representing LEAP Scores of Mr. X

From table 10, it is evident that the subject has scored **22, 20, 18 and 12 in the Director, Coach, Entrepreneur and the Specialist** dimensions of leadership style respectively, with highest being the Director score.

Referring to Figure 10, it is evident that the subject is a **Director** and tends to resort to Director style of leadership in most of the situations, since his/her scoring is the highest (30%) in the Director dimension. The subject can also resort to Coaching (27%) and Entrepreneurship (25%) mode of leadership if the situation demands, as these are his/her secondary scores.

Being more of a Director, the subject **maintains systems** so that operations run in synchrony and order. Moreover, he/she is likely to take a **mentoring stance** to motivate and guide others to follow the established systems and procedures. He/she may define goals and organize resources in an attempt to get the most **cost-effective input** towards the **achievement of goals**. In this manner, the subject is likely to communicate the standards to be met, conveying what is and is not acceptable. The subject aspires to **attain high levels of teamwork, cooperation, consensus** and **commitment** and therefore, takes great initiative in coaching people towards the desired result. The subject would also **invest in developing the team's skills** by providing regular feedback.

Also having a **secondary style of Entrepreneurial approach**, he/she also **tends to place value on ideas, change and innovation** and may be **driven for continuous improvement, expansion** and **development for the function or department**. He/she would therefore, strive to use their ideas and those of others to improve existing frameworks, thereby increasing efficiency of operations.

BAT 2 Discussion: LEAP and CPA

Director	Coach	Entrepreneur	Specialist
22	20	18	12
Advise	**Criticize**	**Empathize**	**Searching**
18	2	10	15

Referring to the above tables and graphs, it is seen that subject "X" primarily resorts to a Directorial style of leadership, the secondary one being the Coach, followed by the Entrepreneur and the last being a Specialist. Also, the subject tends to **resort to advising** primarily while communicating and tends to **ask relevant question** to understand a situation, followed by empathising and the last being criticising.

Being more of a Director, the subject "X" maintains systems so that each operation runs in synchrony and order. Moreover, he/she would often take the **role of an advisor** while communicating, guiding others to follow the established systems and procedures. In this manner, the subject is likely to **communicate the standards** to be met, conveying what is and is not acceptable.

The subject generally tends to mentor his/her people, stressing on motivating and developing their skills by **providing regular feedback.** He/she aspires to attain **high levels of teamwork, cooperation,**

consensus and commitment. In addition, the subject **rarely takes a judgmental stand** on issues which helps him/her maintain a **neutral perspective.** As a result, the team members/peers perceive him/her as an approachable individual with whom they can freely share their views without having the fear of being evaluated and judged.

Being rather entrepreneurial in his/her approach, the subject also tends to **place value on ideas, change and innovation** and may be driven for **continuous improvement, expansion and development** for his/her function or department. The subject would therefore, strive to use his/her ideas and those of others to improve existing frameworks, thereby increasing efficiency of operations.

The subject has a **tendency to probe by asking relevant questions** and may **explore possibilities to find out information** one needs to take things forward. This further helps the subject gain an understanding of the situation from a **holistic perspective.** However, he/she may not consciously try to **understand the perspectives** of others while communicating with them, preferring to advise instead. All the same, not merely focusing on his/her contribution to the organization, he/she leads by **utilizing and integrating the experience**, skills and talents of the team members.

The Verdict

Every individual needs an objective battery of psychometric analysis of their inherent strengths and capabilities to ensure progress and growth in all arenas of life.

The discussion indicates that the background of psychological knowledge obtained from single/independent instruments is less comprehensive as the knowledge obtained when Battery of Psychometric Assessments is applied. Therefore, the Battery of Psychometric Analysis is a holistic approach by scientifically measuring the hidden strengths and discovering opportunities for self-progress and immediate growth possibilities. Clarity and self-awareness helps enhance performance competency from within. Battery of Psychometric assessments act as an INFLUENCING AGENT of CHANGE by valuing this Unique and Holistic evaluation approach in applying the Battery of Psychometric Assessments.

Authors Note

While we have reached the end of the H.A.P.P.Y. book, it must be reiterated that to be HAPPY is your birth-right and happiness should never really end. Here's hoping we have inspired you to take control of your lives and wellbeing, envisioning your happiness and creating it through informed decisions.

On that note, as you are on the adventure of discovering happiness, we would love to help you navigate through life and find it. The key that you seek lies in The Assessment World. To get there, take the Right decision and walk straight on into www.theassessmentworld.com or email us at reach4help@theassessmentworld.com or call us at **+ 91-9972301145.**

Annexure

The Witness Stand

Psychometric Assessment and Its Impact on Human Resource Practices

Owen Fernandés, School of Management/City University of Seattle in Trenčín (2015)

Competencies have become a prime deciding factor in human resource practices. To assess competency in individuals, many assessment centres use a variety of techniques to great effect. Focusing on personality traits, cognitive ability and judging performance during the screening process are common methods. In spite of this, attrition rates are difficult to lower in many organizations and that puts the HR department into a dilemma whether to use or not to use an assessment centre and psychology-based tests. This paper made an effort to highlight some effective and not so effective ways of using assessments to see that the 'best fit' individual is chosen for any given position of work. The article concluded by stressing that it is not always necessary for employers to stick rigidly to psychometric assessment while taking decisions related to human resource practices. It is necessary to choose the best test by combining the traditional approaches and psychometrics. The test is required to fulfil every criterion of a choice of the best tool and it also must be customized according to the given role or given situation. Therefore, the author concluded that the effectiveness of psychometric assessment relies on its combination with the other techniques and that it is required to be a part of the recruitment process and not as the only criteria in recruitment process.

'Current Recruitment and Selection Practises: A National Survey of Fortune 1000 Firms'

Chris Piotrowski, Terry Armstrong (2006)

This study reported the findings of survey data on recruitment and pre-employment selection methods used by human resource departments in major companies in USA. In addition, data on use of online pre-employment tests were collected. The analysis was based on responses from 151 firms. The findings indicated that the majority of companies rely on traditional recruitment and personnel selection techniques over the use of online assessment instruments. It was also found that personality testing is popular in about 20% of the firms and one fifth of the respondents plan to implement online testing in the future. Furthermore, screening for honesty-integrity (28.5%) and violence potential (22%) was found to be somewhat popular.

The Big Five Personality Dimensions and Job Performance: A Meta-Analysis

Murray R. Barrick, Michael K. Mount (1991)

A study investigated the relation of the "Big Five" personality dimensions to three job performance criteria – job proficiency, training proficiency and personnel data, for five occupational groups – professionals, police, managers, sales, and skilled/semi-skilled. Results indicated that Conscientiousness showed consistent relations with all job performance criteria for all occupational groups. Extraversion was a valid predictor across criterions for two occupations involving interaction – managers and sales. Also, Openness to Experience and Extraversion were significant predictors of the training proficiency criterion.

Future Trend for Research

While there are some notable studies conducted on the usage of psychometrics, there remains a research gap in studying the effectiveness of a battery of assessments. The reason could be that different psychometric assessments are owned by different individual organisations/entities. Sometimes, even the different versions of the same psychometric assessment, measuring the same factor are owned by different organisations. This in turn may make it very difficult to combine assessments in the behavioural interpretation which may not give a holistic/complete picture.

The book intends to highlight the value and the importance of **H**olistic **A**pproach to **P**ersonality, **P**sychometrics and **Y**ou. It stresses on how combining the multiple battery of assessments from a common source can help in understanding individuals of various walks of life and organisations in totality to move towards the path of success, growth and progress.

The Stories We Promised

The following case studies are an elaborated discussion of the case snippets mentioned in an earlier chapter. These cases help explain the use and benefit of psychometric assessments in various situations.

Case Study 1: Succession Planning

Problem Statement –

A company was weighing two employees at the managerial level in the department of Accounts for the position of Deputy General Manager of Accounts and Costing department. The candidates were to be assessed on competencies and abilities such as critical analysis, maintenance of records and preparing audit reports, maintaining relationships with stakeholders, training team, implementation of management initiatives and such, to suggest the best suitable candidate for the promotion.

Recommendation to solve the problem stated –

The candidates were instructed to take up a Battery of 4 Assessments to understand their inherent personality (FITS), the influence of environment (4Cs), communication patterns (CPA) and the current competencies (PPC20) of the individual. In addition to the assessment interpretations, skills required for the role were referred to from the Job Description and the background details of both the potential candidates such as their current key responsibility areas.

Case study/Analysis –

JD, BAT 4 (FITS, 4Cs, CPA & PPC20) scores and the background details of the 2 potential candidates were considered while suggesting the suitable candidate for the promotion to the Deputy General Manager of Accounts and Costing department.

According to the holistic analysis/report, the **2nd candidate** was suggested to be the most suitable candidate for the promotion.

- **FITS** Scores suggest he/she is an **Intuitor (30.5)** primarily and secondly a **Thinker** (28.5) & a **Feeler (26.5)**

- **4Cs** suggests he/she is a **Conforming (29), Consistent (25.5)** person – thereby being a **Passive Responder (54.5)** and a **Task – Oriented** (52) person

- **CPA** scores suggests that his/her communicating style is that of **Advising (16)**, **Empathising (15)** and **Searching**

- **PPC20** suggests that he/she is **good** at Relationships (6), at Motivating others (7), at Oral Communication (6), taking Initiatives (6), Planning (6), Quality Focus (6) and has good Learning Orientation (6) and Business Awareness (7). It can be seen that he/she has **moderate** scores in areas like Risk Taking (5), Innovation (5), Flexibility (4), Analytical Thinking (5), Sensitivity (5), Teamwork (4), Achievement (4), Authority/ Presence (4) and Resilience (5). He/she has **low** scores in areas like Decision Making (3), Customer Focus (3) and Developing People (3). These low scores can pose problems to him/her and also for those around at times and it's an indication for him/her to develop on these competencies.

With an inherent inclination towards emotions, ideas and rational thinking, he/she exhibits a host of strengths, and he/she can use these strengths in his favour. He/she can generate ideas and has the ability to validate the same, bearing in mind others' needs and their responses. Thus, he/she considers multiple perspectives, novelty, people and results.

His/her strength lies in being able to formulate the big picture and quickly connecting the dots, based on available data. With the ability to grasp information quickly, he/she not only would be able to understand things at a broader, conceptual level but also get into the crux of the matter. Hence, he/she could be counted on to identify issues and resolve them, providing multiple options to choose from. His/her pragmatic orientation would guide him/her to creating systematic plans and proposals, which would help the Accounts team to perform with better understanding of the function.

As an individual with an analytical bent of mind, he/she would support his decisions with logic. Working methodically, he/she enjoys tasks that utilize his/her expertise and allows him/her to produce positive results. He/she tends to maintain the status quo of the environment, not wanting to upset the existing balance. Thus, he/she may hesitate to take the plunge, until he/she is certain of the favourability of the situation.

Preferring to remain within his/her comfort zone, he/she sticks to what he/she knows best. Within his area of specialization, he/she may be open to trying out new techniques and methods to take advantage of opportunities and obtain better results. As a keen learner, he/she is geared towards continuous improvement and makes use of the available resources to enhance his/her knowledge and skillsets.

He/she comes across as a friendly and approachable individual, who is inclined towards helping others and addressing their concerns when required. Caring and considerate, he/she places great importance on the needs & feelings of others, with the objective of being a strong support system in their time of need. As an approachable individual, people do not hesitate to come to him/her for advice. With his/her communication skills, he/she conveys his/her point across clearly & concisely to others. Seldom using critical response in his/her conversations, he/she would take efforts to make communication a two-way process.

He/she would also be keen to motivate people to put their best foot forward and empower them to reach their potential. Therefore, his/her interpersonal skills indicate that he/she can work with internal cross functional teams and interact easily with external customers. He/she is likely to enjoy work that allows him/her to be in control, follow through with plans, and see expected results, preferring a degree of structure & predictability.

Keeping in consideration past experiences, future events and present situations, he/she learns from each experience and is interested on continuous improvement. He/she tends to lead by setting an example for others, thus, allowing his/her professional work to speak for itself, coming across as grounded. Taking initiative, within his/her comfort zone, he/she can lead his team through a variety of situations, tackling issues as and when they arise.

His/Her business awareness would be a value add when looking to leverage on the market position of the organisation. He/she is inclined to keep abreast with the rules/regulations pertaining to compliance of statutory requirement of the paper industry. Hence, he/she has the potential to use this knowledge to design and develop financial strategies that would help the organization sustain its growth. Nevertheless, putting these into action may take time, with him/her preferring to consider all perspectives beforehand.

While he/she has a host of strengths to his/her credit, he/she may like to look at some of the areas if he/she wants to leverage his/her full potential. Not being inherently action-oriented, he/she may have a challenge in converting his/her ideas into concrete plans and accomplishing results at a fast pace. His/Her tendency to take time to arrive at decisions could also be a point of concern when looking to leverage on opportunities to accelerate accounting/costing operations. Also, coupled with his/her flexible sense of urgency, he/she prefers long-term assignments requiring calculated responses and working in an even-paced, consistent style. Working in a methodical manner, he/she may take up one thing at a time.

With the above understanding, the 2nd candidate has the inherent potential and possesses many competencies to give his/her best in the day-to-day activities. With people being the key to the success of any organization, responding quickly to internal/external customers and involving his/her team members in decision making to nurture his/her team as a part of interpersonal effectiveness would be a critical determinant of his/her personal & professional accomplishments. He/she may need to improve in the areas of decision making, customer focus (internal/external) and developing people to be effective in his/her role. Hence, with appropriate grooming, he/she may be considered as a potential candidate for the position of DGM-Accounts & Costing.

Case Study 2: Team Profiling

Problem Statement –

A client wanted to gauge how a team of 6 people from an organisation functioned collaboratively as leaders. The client wanted to understand what the team members' strengths and challenges are and identify how each member's skills could supplement another's shortcoming.

Recommendation to solve the problem stated –

The team had taken a Battery of 4 assessments – FITS, 4Cs, CPA and PPC20. The battery gauged their innate potentials, behaviours, motivators and stressors, communication patterns and current competencies. The individual scores were consolidated and interpreted according to nine parameters provided by the client. The nine parameters were: Process, Strategic Direction, Relationships, Team Work, Customer Orientation, Commitment to Purpose, Internal Communication, External Communication and Resilience.

Case study/Analysis –

To arrive at a singular score denoting where the team stands on each parameter, certain scores of different components of the 4 different assessments were collated for everyone, as mentioned below:

1. **Strategic Direction:** Intuitor + Sensor + Controlling + Task-Oriented + Advising + Searching + Initiative + Risk Taking + Innovation + Decision Making + Planning + Quality Focus +

Achievement + Business Awareness + Learning Orientation + Authority/Presence + Resilience

2. **Process:** Thinker + Controlling + Conforming + Passive Responder + Task-Oriented + Advising + Searching + (Low) Risk Taking + (Low) Flexibility + Analytical Thinking + Planning + Quality Focus + (Low) Motivating Others + Developing People

3. **Relationships:** Feeler + Convincing + Consistent + People Oriented + Advising + (Low) Criticizing + Empathy + Flexibility + Oral Communication + Sensitivity + Relationships + Customer Focus + Motivating

4. **Team Work:** Feeler + Intuitor + Controlling + Consistent + Balanced TO/PO + Advising + (Low) Criticizing + Empathy + Searching + Initiative + Flexibility + Oral Communication + Relationships + Team Work + Motivating Others + Developing People

5. **Customer Orientation:** Feeler + Convincing + Consistent + Balanced TO/PO + Advising + (Low) Criticizing + Empathy + Searching + Initiative + Innovation + Decision making + Quality Focus + Oral Communication + Sensitivity + Relationships + Customer Focus + Business Awareness + Learning Orientation

6. **Commitment to Purpose:** Intuitor + Thinker + Sensor + Controlling + Consistent + Task Oriented + Active Initiator + Initiative + Innovation + Flexibility + Planning + Achievement + Learning Orientation + Resilience

7. **Internal Communication:** Feeler + Thinker + Convincing + Conforming + Consistent + Balanced TO/PO + (Low) Criticizing + Empathy + Searching + Initiative + Flexibility + Planning + Oral Communication + Sensitivity + Relationships + Developing People

8. **External Communication**: Feeler + Thinker + Controlling + Convincing + Balanced TO/PO + Advising + (Low) Criticizing + Empathy + Searching + Initiative+ Flexibility + Planning + Quality Focus + Oral Communication + Sensitivity + Relationships + Customer Focus + Business Awareness + Authority/Presence

9. **Resilience:** Intuitor + Sensor + Controlling + Task-Oriented + Active Initiator + Initiative + Decision Making + Flexibility + Learning Orientation + Resilience

The following percentages were derived upon statistically treating the data:

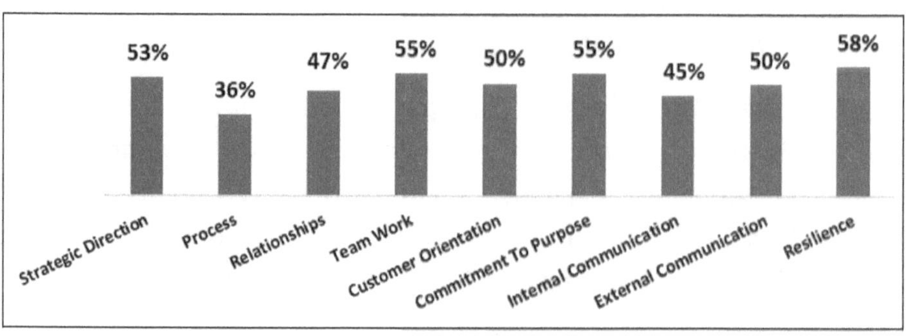

The overall analysis of the parameters is as follows:

1. **Strategic Direction**

Strengths:

- Far sighted and mindful of the bigger picture, the team has the ability to formulate long term goals and exhibit commitment towards its achievement.

- The team is likely to initiate projects, keeping into consideration current business trends and competitors.

- Curious by nature, they are likely to ask questions to gain information, thereby building their knowledge base in order to avoid unnecessary risks. Further, they may also keep a lookout for business opportunities.

- Motivated by quick results, they have the potential to break down long term objectives into short term goals that help track progress.

- Confident and self-assured, the members are likely to motivate each other and collectively put in effort to move towards their goals.

Challenges:

- Satisfied with a cursory review of available data, the team is unlikely to dig for facts and figures to corroborate their propositions.

- Inclined towards creative thinking, the team may not put enough emphasis on critical analysis of the idea thus missing out on the practicality of it.

- Dealing with more than one idea, the team might find it difficult to settle onto one to pursue, delaying decision making

2. **Process**

Strengths:

- Willing to challenge status quo, the team is open to interpreting rules in a flexible manner for organizational benefit.

- Creative and likely to enjoy intellectual challenges, they are eager to test techniques that have not been used traditionally, thereby approach situations from different angles.

Challenges:

- Unlikely to plan out their work prior to execution, they may not prioritize their work in an effective manner, thereby compromising on quality as well as deadlines.

- Not inclined to work within set procedures or adhere to customs, they are likely to posit ideas and techniques that may be conflicting with the organization's policies.

- Unlikely to carry out a detailed analysis of the situation, team may tend to misdiagnose a problem, leading to inappropriate usage of resources to deal with the perceived situation.

3. Relationships

Strengths:

- Coming off as warm and friendly, the team may find it easy to build rapport and maintain group morality and cohesion.

- People oriented by nature, the team is likely to relate well with each other, thereby building a strong working relationship.

- Vocal and expressive, the group is likely to avoid communication gaps and hence remain in touch with the development within the team.

- Intellectually stimulated, the team is likely to have discussions on various topics thereby maintaining constant contact with each other.

Challenges:

- While the team members listen to each other, they are unlikely to consider the views of others or be considerate to their individual thoughts.

- Likely to be direct and straightforward in expressing their opinions, the team may be quick to find faults in others' work and the environment alike, making it difficult in maintaining an optimistic outlook.

- Competitive by nature, the members may try to override the opinions of others, turning constructive debates into conflicts and thereby causing possible rifts between the members.

4. **Team Work**

Strengths:

- Having the ability to articulate, the team is likely to pitch their ideas in an appealing manner to gain the favour of others and help their progress along the way.

- People focused, the team is likely to ensure that everyone is on-board with the ideas before going through with it, reducing chances of contradiction during execution.

- Enjoying people contact, the team has the ability to build a large network of contacts, through which they could potentially fulfil their objectives.

Challenges:

- While debating on a contentious issue the team might get into criticizing each other for any missing link.

- Inclined to accumulate the popular vote, the team may spend too much time on convincing each other of their own ideas thereby delaying the execution and task completion.

- While the team members encourage growth of each other, they may not actively try to foster each other's potential.

5. **Customer Orientation**

Strengths:

- Attuned to emotions, the team members have the ability to understand the feelings of internal as well as external customers, enabling them to establish rapport which supports them in accumulating business networks.

- Seeking approval of their ideas, the team has the ability to express their thoughts with clarity and use a persuasive mode of communication.

- Likely to have a fair understanding of the business and industry; this allows them to provide suitable recommendations to the clients.

- Focusing moderately on strengths and weaknesses, the team has potential to learn from its previous experience and prevent repetition, which in turn helps them deal with customer issues more efficiently.

Challenges:

- Driven towards overcoming challenges, the team is likely to push their opinions that may lead to confrontations.

- In a quest to be different, the team is likely to find alternatives to solve customer related issues. This might prove difficulty in making quick decisions, causing delay in deadlines.

- Although the team comes across as friendly, it may lack a positive approach towards providing recommendations and form biased opinions.

- Focused on gaining a holistic perspective, the team is unlikely to delve into details and compromise quality of the tasks delivered.

6. **Commitment to Purpose**

Strengths:

- Driven towards futuristic goals, the team has the potential to take charge of the situation and actively seek to face obstacles coming across as an ambitious team.

- Motivated to achieve results and stay on top, they have the potential to step out of the comfort zone and bring about new initiatives. Further, the team also has the willingness to adapt to new situations and work through challenges, being flexible to the environmental influences.

- Team has the potential to generate various alternative solutions, coming across as creative problem solvers.

Challenges:

- While they are competitive, the team may not prefer to work at a steady pace thereby finding it difficult to work with persistence.

- With a tendency to work based on spontaneity, they are not likely to follow a systematic method of operation. Their lack of planning could also lead to taking on projects without a thorough assessment and may lead to wastage of resources.

- Although the team has the potential to deal with setbacks and the grit to face situations, anxious to please customers, they may find it hard to deal with adverse circumstances.

7. **Internal Communication**

Strengths:

- Likely to enjoy expression of their ideas, the team tends to proactively seek social interaction, having the potential to promote a friendly work environment.

- Displaying conviction and curiosity, they have the potential to draw out the concerns of their team members and provide suggestions based on the same.

- With a bent towards curiosity, the team members have the potential to draw out key information thereby remaining abreast of the team's progress.

Challenges:

- Anxious to impress others, the team members are likely to emphasize on their individual ideas, with a tendency to override their colleagues, leading to feelings of dissatisfaction.

- With a tendency to focus on the errors, a lack of positive appraisal could cause frustration within the team.

- Likely to question authority, they might find it challenging to stick to conventions and set standards. Thus, a lack of structure could interrupt an organized flow of communication.

8. **External Communication**

Strengths:

- Inclined towards the desire to win acceptance of others, the team has the potential to verbalize their ideas in a compelling manner to gain stakeholders' buy-in.

- With an inclination to deal with impromptu situations, the team also has the ability to derive creative solutions in the nick of time, potentially creating a positive impact on their clients.

- Having a fair understanding of their customers' needs, the team has the ability to gauge their requirements and work towards it by getting to the bottom of the issue.

Challenges:

- Likely to lack planning and not getting into details, the team might miss out on providing key information revolving around critical concerns of the client.

- Further, eager to provide suggestions, they might not be attentive to the client's point of view which could lead to misunderstandings.

- The team members are also inclined towards noticing the errors and faults of the other party, rather than appraising the situation positively, which may lead to loss of business opportunities.

9. **Resilience**

Strengths:

- Inclined towards taking charge of a situation and energized by overcoming barriers, the team is likely to tackle a stressful situation confidently.

- Exhibiting an inclination towards spontaneity, they have the ability to think quickly to respond to unforeseen obstacles.

- Inherently creative, the team has the potential to deal with taxing circumstances by coming up with alternative solutions.

Challenges:

- While the team shows potential to retain composure under moderate levels of stress, they may buckle under excessive strain due to low resilience.

- Likely to approach a problem head on, the lack of a structured plan of action may land the team into avoidable problems.

- Trying to work with multiple ideas at once, the team may not be able to decide on a single course of action which could prove to be stressful.

- The lack of a logical backup of their ideas and their tendency to buckle under pressure could possibly lead the team to take impractical decisions that might hinder progress further.

Recommendation

As a team of inherently creative members with a focus on the larger perspective, they have the potential to focus on generating ideas that facilitates the achievement of long term goals. Enjoying people contact, they come across as a team of friendly members with the ability to build a large network using their potential persuasive skills.

Likely to focus on the bigger picture, they have a tendency to overlook minor details which may compromise the quality of the tasks delivered. Being spontaneous, the team is likely to avoid meticulous planning and prioritization, leaving things to last minute which could lead to wastage of resources.

With a tendency to provide recommendations, the team may provide readymade solutions. Taking an appreciative stance by incorporating others' points of view, the team can enhance performance by providing positive feedback rather than taking a criticizing approach.

As a team of varied strengths, leveraging on the individual as well as the group talents can help them stay ahead of their challenges.

In addition, collaborating with individuals with strengths that counterbalance possible blind-spots, the team can increase their productivity and achieve their objectives.

Case Study 3: Recruitment

Problem Statement –

The Managing Director of an automotive company "X" faced an issue in deciding the best candidate out of 3 highly eligible candidates.

Recommendation to solve the problem stated –

Most recruiters face a similar issue in making a call on the most suitable candidate from the best of the lot. In such situations, psychometric assessments are aligned with the job description along with the resume of the candidates to provide a comprehensive understanding of the subtle indicators of their behaviours. For example, job hopping behaviour can be drawn from the details of work experience of the candidate. Thus, the competencies of the candidates are not the sole indicators in making decisions.

The 3 candidates were instructed to take up a Battery of 5 Assessments to help understand inherent personality, the influence of environment, communication and behaviour patterns and the current competencies of the individual – all of which are interpreted from a holistic perspective to provide a comprehensive understanding. These scores, along with the JD and the resumes of the candidates were considered holistically in analysing the right fit for the right job.

Case study/Analysis –

Resumes, JD and the BAT 5 (FITS, 4Cs, CPA, BPA & PPC20) scores of all the three candidates were considered while suggesting the right candidate for the decided designation – Corporate Head – Supply Chain Management for the organisation "X."

According to the holistic analysis/report, the **3rd candidate** was suggested to be the right fit for the current opening offered in the organisation.

- **FITS** Scores suggest he/she is a **Thinker (29.5)** primarily and secondly an **Intuitor (23.5)**

- **4Cs** suggests he/she is a **Controlling (28), Conforming (24)** person – thereby being **Active Initiator (51), People Oriented (51) and Passive Responder (49) & Task Oriented (49)**

- **CPA** scores suggests that his/her communicating style is that of **Searching (19)** and **Advising (17)**

- **BPA** scores suggests that he/she is flexible when it comes to communicating off work but is moderately outspoken when it comes to communicating at work, is moderately extrovert at work and extremely extrovert off work, has a flexible sense of urgency at work and moderately low sense of urgency off work and is extremely systematic in processing information both at work and off work

- **PPC20** suggests that he/she is good at Team Work (6), at Taking Initiatives (7), Achievement (7) & Decision Making (7), Planning (7), Sensitivity (7), makes his/her Presence Felt (7) and has good Resilience (6). He/she has over strength in areas like Relationships (8) Innovation (9), Quality Focus (8), Oral Communication (9), Customer Focus (8), Business Awareness (10), Learning Orientation (9) Motivating Others (8) and Developing People (9). These over strengths can pose problems to him/her and also for those around at times. Also, it can be seen that he/she has moderate scores in areas like analytical thinking (5), flexibility (5). The subject doesn't have any low score in the 20 competencies except for risk taking (3), which denotes, he/she has worked on improving his/her competency over the areas and also shows his/her drive to grow and learn continuously.

Considering the above, it is seen that this candidate being organized, idea-driven and result-oriented individual, comes across as a person who would validate his/her ideas to form an objective outlook of situations, rational in his/her approach and maximize results in supply chain operations. Working methodically, he/she enjoys tasks that utilize his/her expertise and allow him/her to produce positive outcomes. Setting detailed plans in place, he/she would delve into the finer aspects to ensure high quality levels in his/her work while adhering to the set timeline. Being inherently inclined towards analysis, he/she may sieve through information and get into details with systematic approach. This enables him/her to zero-in on key issues and make logical decisions. All the same, as a pragmatic individual in his/her method, he/she may also prefer to be intuitive to accomplish his/her job.

He/she also has the inherent ability to generate and validate a host of ideas that would prove useful when expected to solve problems. His/her inquisitive nature coupled with his/her capability to grasp concepts quickly enables him/her to obtain a holistic view of company's operations. He/she has the innate potential to think out of the box which allows him/her to generate a variety of alternatives to tackle challenges with both a creative as well as logical problem-solving methods. Possessing the ability to approach situations from multiple angles, he/she would be able to come up with a range of possibilities to resolve supply chain management issues.

His/her developed interpersonal skills would allow him/her to build his/her network and act as an interface/support with peers/customers/suppliers/vendors with ease. As an expressive individual, he/she is capable of drawing others' attention and conveying his/her thoughts in a convincing style to wield influence over them. This could help him/her to handle internal collaboration and enable him/her to build a strong customer service level. Negotiating the terms of the deal with the concerned parties, he/she has the potential to gain their buy-in while establishing internal/external benchmark process for procurement. Furthermore, in terms of client interactions, he/she would go out of the way to deliver services that will delight the customer and gain their loyalty.

Taking initiative, he/she can lead his/her team through a variety of situations, relying on his/her interpersonal skills to handle issues. He/she works hard and strives to make a mark in his/her profession, displaying drive and resilience. As a competitive and ambitious person, he/she works hard and desires to make a mark in his/her profession. Being a natural problem-solver, he/she tends to take up challenging goals with enthusiasm. As a keen learner, he/she is prepared towards continuous improvement and can go out of his/her comfort zone to seek resources to enhance his/her knowledge and skillsets in his/her area of work.

As a strategic leader, he/she is motivated to organize change. He/she is focused on results and wants to be productive, competent and influential. Exuding an air of authority and confidence, he/she can get things done through his/her team. Delegating tasks, he/she would empower his team members to meet high quality standards for supplier performance, providing opportunities to achieve their objectives. He/she also nurtures their potential by sharing regular feedback and mentoring. With the drive to stay on top of market dynamics, he/she keeps abreast with the commercial & technology trends and achieve cost savings targets. Analysing various business strategies, he/she strives to differentiate his/her company and gain a competitive advantage by designing robust supply chain solutions based on customer requirement.

Having said the above, his/her over-strength scores on most competencies may also have unfavourable implications. In aspects like Innovation, Analytical thinking, Planning, Quality Focus, Teamwork, Customer Focus, Motivating Others and Developing People, he/she may need to capitalize on his/her abilities while also addressing his/her potential pitfalls to make the most of every opportunity and accomplish goals successfully.

Moreover, his/her overemphasis on explaining the task may find him/her taking control of the conversation. In this process, he/she may not actively listen to others' point of view. Also, with a pointed focus on the task at hand, his/her listening skills may be limited to understanding what others are doing. Thereby, without truly gauging the challenges they may be experiencing and the resultant feelings.

In general, the 3rd candidate can come up with sourcing strategy based on Business Plan and development of vendor management to provide supply chain support to the organisation. He/she can also manage procurement supplier's relationship and ensure supplier performance to meet high quality standards. He/she has the inherent potential and possesses the competency to perform well & gives his/her best for the job role. However, he/she must be aware of his/her over-strengths and its challenges. Thus, he/she comes across as a strong performer and may be considered as a potential candidate for the role of Corporate Head – Supply Chain Management.

Case Study 3: Coaching

Problem Statement –

A global production-based industry had acquired a local manufacturing company. This industry's agenda was to unite the local employees and their own employees to bring about a unified culture. To do so, they were considering an employee from another region to be promoted as the CEO to bring about cohesiveness among the employees. Their expectations included that this new CEO should be capable of bringing harmony and leading the newly formed company towards growth. The position thus requires a leader who can build and maintain effective relations and follow strategic planning to bring in profits.

Recommendation to solve the problem stated –

The candidate was instructed to take up a Battery of 5 Assessments to understand inherent personality (FITS), the influence of environment (4Cs), communication (CPA) and behaviour patterns (BPA) and the current competencies (PPC20) of the individual. The candidate also underwent intensive reflective sessions with a coach and change agent to bring about optimized success for the individual as well as the organization.

Case study/Analysis –

To tap into the candidate's potential and give his/her the best every day, he/she needs to know his/her own true strengths and capabilities. Understanding his/her own hidden potential will enable him/her to strategically invest his/her time, energy and resources into capitalising his/her strengths to fulfil his/her goals and succeed in every aspect of life.

The objective of this coaching intervention is to provide the candidate a holistic view into one's own personality and help him/her to understand oneself better. Obtaining a complete picture of one's personality requires evaluating the same from multiple angles. Thus, the results discussed in this analysis are based on the candidate's responses to the 5 psychometric tools – FITS, 4Cs, BPA (Behaviour Pattern Analysis), CPA (Communication Pattern Analysis) & PPC20 (People Performance Competency 20). This coaching intervention was proposed to help the candidate gain clarity regarding his/her personality, attitudes and behaviours holistically, highlighting the candidates overall strengths and areas of improvement which would help him/her to arrive at actionable steps to address his/her growth and development.

The following analysis would not only help the candidate to gain insight into his/her own personality but also allows the candidate to:

- Recognise the influence of innate factors on interpersonal dynamics

- Gauge the personality styles and preferences of others based on his/her behaviour

- Discover ways to flex one's communication to match the wavelength of other people

- Identify one's behaviour patterns across different contexts and situations

- Enhance one's personal and professional effectiveness by understanding individual differences

According to the holistic analysis and the reflective sessions held, the following were the findings.

- **FITS** Scores suggest he/she is a **Feeler (30.5)** primarily and secondly an **Intuitor (26.5)**

- **4Cs** suggests he/she is a **Consistent (28), Controlling (26) & a Convincing (26)** person – thereby being an **Active Initiator (52)** and a **People – Oriented (54)** person

- **CPA** scores suggests that his/her communicating style is that of **Searching (19), Empathising (14)** & **Advising (12)**

- BPA scores suggests that he/she is moderately outspoken when it comes to communicating at work but is moderately diplomatic when it comes to communicating off work, is moderately extrovert at work and flexible off work, has a moderately low sense of urgency at work and a flexible sense of urgency off work and is moderately systematic in processing information at work and flexible in processing information off work

- **PPC20** suggests that he/she is good at Relationships (7), at Oral Communication (7), at Motivating Others (7), at Taking Initiatives (7), Customer Focus (6), makes his/her Presence Felt (6), has good Resilience (7) and Learning Orientation (7). It can be seen that he/she has moderate scores in areas like Risk Taking (5), Innovation (5), Analytical Thinking (4), Decision Making (5), Planning (4), Quality Focus (4), Sensitivity (5), Developing People (5) and Business Awareness (5). He/she has low scores in Achievement (3). The candidate has over strengths in areas like Flexibility (8) and Team Work (8). These low and over strength scores can pose problems to him/her and also for those around at times and it's an indication for him/her to work on these competencies.

Innately emotional, the candidate tends to be attuned to the moods and feelings of others and relate with his/her colleagues. Sensitive to people's concerns and willing to lend a helping hand to those in need, he/she comes across as a responsive and supportive individual. His/her ability to empathise with their problems and express the same in his/her communication enables him/her to make others feel understood and valued, leading to stronger bonds.

Idea driven by nature, he/she tends to come up with a range of alternatives to any situation, exploring different routes to address issues. His/her creative bent of mind is also evident in his/her proclivity to try out novel methods and approaches in the pursuit of improvement. Thus, he/she is not afraid to challenge status quo and bring in different systems if they could serve as effective tools to achieve results. Staying updated with industry developments and strives to find profitable avenues to enhance business outcomes for the organisation.

Seeking intellectual stimulation, he/she enjoys working on challenging assignments, and is not easily bogged down by setbacks. Instead, he/she relies on his/her ingenuity and resourcefulness to obtain positive outcomes. As a keen learner, he/she is eager to address his/her development, seeking regular feedback and reflecting on his/her experiences to derive meaningful lessons from his/her past. He/she is also inclined to make the most of learning opportunities, proactively utilizing time and resources to add his/her growth. He/she may bring about development within his/her teams through frequent training and coaching activities. Hence, he/she make an effort to obtain optimum performance from them.

As a leader, he/she shares his/her vision with his/her team, to provide clarity on the overall goals as well as acquire their buy-in. Articulate and assertive in communication, his/her strengths lie in influencing others and helping them to see his/her perspective. His/her decisions are typically democratic, involving inputs from key stakeholders and team members, and giving due importance to group consensus. In this manner, he/she tends to maintain healthy relationships with people, understanding the importance of creating win-win situations for all parties involved.

Adaptable with different kinds of people and situations, he/she keeps interactions friendly and pleasant. With the ability to act as a mediator, he/she looks for ways to minimise conflict, thereby harmonizing team efforts. While he/she is assertive and generally knows where to draw the line, in the effort to maintain harmony, he/she may sometimes find himself/herself giving in to others. This could potentially hamper business goals, and he/she may, at times, be taken advantage of by others.

Inquisitive and quick to grasp information, he/she tends to have a broad understanding of several topics. This aids him/her in establishing rapport and easily connecting with a diverse array of people.

Managing his/her team members through effective delegation allows him/her to focus on the broader goals while they take care of the finer details of execution. With the faith in his/her team's potential, he/she tend to ask questions to understand the status of ongoing projects, he/she may consider asking more pertinent and specific questions to help him/her arrive at the root cause of issues.

Not innately driven towards action, he/she may be inclined to take time to kick-start initiatives, he/she may get caught up in the exploration and conceptualization of the issue, as various options may seem appealing. Thus, may lead to delays on occasion, where he/she may find himself or herself in a rush to meet targets. Moreover, although he/she can cope with stress, he/she tends to work at a steady pace and may dislike working under intense pressure, preferring to maintain a balance between his/her personal and professional space. He/she could consider drawing up clear, detailed plans that would help him/her organise upcoming projects and deliver as per set timeline. While he/she looks to achieve results, he/she may exhibit a high sense of urgency or push his/her people to reach targets, facing additional delays. Therefore, he/she could consider working with individuals who are naturally action-oriented, as they may serve as a catalyst in helping him/her speed up team efforts towards the end goal.

Geared towards self-growth and development, he/she has the potential to capitalize on his/her inherent strengths and address his/her shortcomings to achieve personal and professional success in his/her life, career and relationships.

The assessment results have provided evidence of his/her strengths and opportunities for development. As a leader, he/she has a balanced and appropriate attitude and demeanour in all situations, treating others with respect. Actively embraces different situations as they arise in a positive way and promotes learning from mistake. He/she creates an environment where others are encouraged to innovate and openly recognise efforts of his/her team. Targeting areas for development will allow him/her to strengthen his/her leadership profile.

Stated below were some of the additional suggestions for the candidate to cultivate and transit from a leadership to executive position.

To help him/her optimise his/her success, the candidate was encouraged to put effort in developing a strategic outlook. At the individual level, it would require him/her to constantly evaluate new ways to update, improve, and refine processes and services to reach target customers and business goals.

To think in strategic terms about innovative solutions/and or emerging organisation, the candidate was suggested to:

- Think beyond the work environment and make decision in the context of the bigger picture

- Actively increase one's knowledge/awareness of the business and competitive environment to determine long-term, problems or opportunities

- Develop and establish broad scale, longer-term objectives, goals or projects (i.e. affecting a function or department)

- Examine business needs in an attempt to identify opportunities or obstacles. Learn to let go of the past and look beyond present and future opportunities

- Analyse complex business issues and distil new solutions which are consistent with the strategy and vision

- Astutely identify trends and make linkages between issues and potential opportunities that are not obvious to others

- Develop new concepts, adapt current solutions and implement innovative approaches to meet emerging business needs

Case Study 4: Career Mapping

Problem Statement –

A 21-year-old student, who had completed his/her bachelor's in business and Management, faced the challenge of choosing a career. He/she had gained work experience by working with event companies and various other MNCs as a sales person as well as a host/hostess. Before deciding on a career, he/she wanted to gauge his/her strengths and challenges, and depending on them, determine a career path that would suit his/her the best.

Recommendation to solve the problem stated –

The candidate was instructed to take up a Battery of 4 Assessments to understand his/her inherent personality (FITS), the influence of environment (4Cs), learning style preference (CARS) and Multiple Intelligences (MI) to help him/her choose the right career that suits him/her.

Case study/Analysis –

The Psychometric tools used are a powerful combination of hereditary and environmental measures, gauging the individual's personality and learning styles on a holistic level. A result of commendable research, these assessments provide individuals with an objective framework that will enable them to choose the right path to continue growing and learning based on their potentials and strengths. The following Battery of 4 psychometric assessments gives a comprehensive insight into the candidate's strength and potential.

According to the holistic analysis/report, the following were the findings:

- **FITS** scores suggest he/she is a **Feeler (32.5)** primarily and secondly an **Intuitor (24.5)**

- **4Cs** suggests he/she is a **Consistent (29), Conforming (28)** person – thereby being a **Passive Responder (57), Task – Oriented (50) and a People Oriented (50)** person

- **CARS** suggest that he/she processes information in an **Abstract Random fashion (32)** primarily and in a **Concrete Sequential (28)** fashion

- **MI** suggests that the subject has high scores in areas like **Interpersonal Intelligence (21), Rhythmic Intelligence (19), Visual (19), Kinesthetic (20), Intrapersonal (18) and Metaphysical Intelligence (20).**

Strengths of the Candidate:

- **Determined** – With an ability to work with long-term projects and plans, he/she is likely to work towards his/her goals steadily. This enables him/her tends look at his/her plans through and attain his/her objectives

- **Process Oriented** – Comfortable working with traditional procedures, he/she tends to use tried and tested methods that have stood the test of time. This ensures he/she achieves guaranteed results

- **Organised** – Preferring to work within a structure, he/she is likely to follow guidelines and maintain expected standards of quality. This helps him/her deliver accurate and precise results

- **Accommodating** – With an inclination to maintain harmony in a group, he/she is open to the views of others while taking decisions, thereby facilitating cohesion. This also leads to co-operative relationships, and he/she is likely to be perceived as warm and approachable

- **Friendly** – Enjoying people interaction, he/she tends to be interactive and social. Thus, he/she is likely to enjoy being surrounded by a large circle of friends, equipping him/her with emotional support

- **Caring** – With the ability to pick up on emotional cues, he/she responds to others in a considerate manner. Thus, he/she is likely to offer support and comfort when people need it, coming across as affectionate

- **Obedient** – Holding authority in high esteem, he/she may carry out the tasks delegated to him/her in a dutiful manner. Operating in the domain of ethics, he/she respects implicit norms and traditions. Hence, he/she is likely to abide by values and his/her belief systems, coming across as disciplined

Motivators of the Candidate:

- Structured environment where rules and instructions are clearly mentioned

- Meeting set expectations and standards of quality

- Harmonious and supportive environment

- Supervision and regular feedback to ensure if proceeding on the right track

- Reassurance from authority figures and respect from those held in regard

- Opportunity to pace work according to own comfort

Stressors of the Candidate:

- Ambiguous instructions and/or unstructured environments

- Conflicts and confrontation in relations

- Failure to meet expectations or deadlines

- Taking decisions that go against the consent of senior members

- Challenging established rules

Blind Spots of the Candidate:

- **Decision making** – He/she exhibits a preference for supervision and feedback to ensure that he/she is on the right track. However, this could result in him/her hesitating to take decisions independently.

Going back and forth looking for reassurance may result in delay and compromise deadlines

- **Initiative** – Seeking guidance from an authority figure, he/she may not seize passing opportunities unless pushed towards them. This may result in him/her losing out on beneficial avenues to explore

- **Expression** – With an inclination to remain in the good books of others, he/she may hesitate to express his/her opinions if he/she feels they are contradictory. Thus, he/she may end up bottling his/her feelings, which is likely to take a toll on him/her

- **Logical orientation** – Relying on feelings and overlooking facts, he/she may settle to proceed with others' supporting his/her ideas. Thus, rational evaluation of the situation/ideas may be lacking, compromising objectivity in conclusions

Learning styles of the Candidate:

- Social by nature, he/she tends to learn through interactions. Thus, group activities and discussions are likely to facilitate his/her learning process

- He/she is likely to retain information better if he/she personalises it through real-life examples, as he/she tends to relate learning to an emotional experience

- He/she has the ability to absorb abstract ideas and impressions and reflect on it to derive meaningful insights. This aids consolidation of information and helps one grasp it as well

- He/she has the potential to use his/her imagination to create make-believe situations that support as examples to foster greater understanding of concepts

Multiple Intelligences of the Candidate:

- **Interpersonal Intelligence** – Innately sensitive and feeling oriented, he/she enjoys social contact. He/she has the ability to understand people, communicate effectively, resolve conflicts and such. He/she tends to enjoy group discussions, activities and social gatherings, to name a few.

- **Rhythmic Intelligence** – Having a fairly developed musical ability, he/she has the potential to understand, create and interpret musical pitches timbre and tones. He/she has the capability to pick up sounds, remember melodies and rhythm

- **Intrapersonal Intelligence** – Aware of his/her emotions and moods, he/she may reflect or introspect about his/her experiences to a moderate extent. This enables him/her to gauge his/her strengths and weaknesses, increasing self-awareness

- **Kinesthetic Intelligence** – Having fairly developed motor skills, he/she is likely to be effective in activities that require a firm hand over movement. He/she may enjoy action driven activities, such as sports, using tools, crafts

- **Visual Intelligence** – Observant of one's surroundings, he/she has the potential to work with visual stimuli. With a fairly developed visual intelligence, he/she has the ability to represent information graphically. He/she is likely to enjoy activities such as painting, drawing and solving puzzles

- **Metaphysical Intelligence** – As someone who may enjoy intellectual stimulation, he/she is likely to muse about the cosmos, mythology, existential concepts and such. Interested in the ultimate reality, he/she may enjoy discussions about the same

- **Logical Intelligence** – He/she has the potential to work with data and infer meaning from them. Having a fairly developed mathematical intelligence, he/she has an affinity to work with number, experiment, solve problems and such activities

- **Natural Intelligence** – Though appreciative of nature and all living beings, he/she may not like to be involved with it.

Unlikely to try to work in nature and explore it, he/she may not go out of his/her way to understand or learn about the environment and other natural events

- **Linguistic Intelligence** – Preferring a face-to-face interactional environment, he/she may not enjoy activities such as reading and writing

Future Direction for the Candidate:

The candidate's innate ability to pick up on the moods and needs of people to respond accordingly exhibits his/her effective interpersonal skills. This is likely to facilitate his/her success in the hotel and tourism industry. Guest relations and front office are areas he/she could explore.

His/her educational background and experience, along with his/her ability to identify an approach that is likely to be impactful, would enable him/her to explore the field of sales and marketing. His/her visual and kinesthetic intelligence would also facilitate the same. However, he/she may consider developing and enhancing his/her ability to persuade others to have a successful career in the field of sales and business development.

His/her affinity towards people relations and tendency to work with rules and ethics also opens the field of psychology for the candidate. He/she may also consider the field of human resources and an educator, both roles that involve people management skills.

Case Study 4: Organizational Behaviour Profiling

Problem Statement –

A prestigious organisation was facing a common issue with their entire workforce – the lack of ownership, accountability and responsibility. They felt that their workforce did not have a futuristic outlook and was focused on just today's operations. This hampered the speed of progress towards materialising the organisation's collective vision.

Recommendation to solve the problem stated –

Based on detailed discussions with the organisation's leaders, behavioural interventions were designed to attain the particular objectives of fostering ownership, accountability and responsibility. As part of the process intervention, the participants had taken two psychometric assessments, FITS and PPC. FITS revealed their inherent personality and innate potential while PPC20 marked their current standing in various competencies. This enabled them to gauge the gap between their potentials and current performance. The scores of all the participants across batches were collated and studied.

Case study/Analysis:

Based on a consolidation of FITS and PPC20 scores of 203 participants across batches of the interventions, it was found that:

- The group consisted of 17% Feelers, 33% Intuitors, 37% Thinkers and 13% Sensors.

- As indicated by PPC20, the group fared moderately well in Innovation (5.0), Analytical Thinking (5.0), Planning (5.8), Quality Focus (5.1), Oral Communication (5.3), Business Awareness (5.0), Learning Orientation (5.8) and Motivating Others (5.6). They scored low in Initiative (4.8), Risk Taking (3.7), Flexibility (4.6), Decision Making (3.8), Sensitivity (4.8), Relationship (4.6), Teamwork (4.8), Achievement (4.9), Customer Focus (4.8), Authority (4.2), Developing People (4.5) and Resilience (4.1).

Based on the aforementioned scores, the following analysis was made.

(Thinker + Intuitor + Analytical Thinking + Innovation + Risk Taking + Decision Making)

Driving Change – As a predominantly Thinker – Intuitor group, they display the **potential to critically analyse** events and incorporate innovations to bring about necessary changes. However, as a group that seeks a **sense of security**, they would prefer methodologies that provide evidence of efficacy. Hence, they are **less likely to take risks** to push for results, **limiting their ability to drive changes** that impact the department as a whole. They are likely to invest time in **ensuring predictable outcomes**, thereby **slowing down their speed of decision making**. While this helps them maintain productivity, it inhibits driving competitive changes that could accelerate the organization's growth exponentially.

(Sensor + Achievement + Planning + Quality Focus + Initiative + Authority + Risk Taking + Sensitivity)

Futuristic Thinking – The group is likely to focus on **completion of tasks, as assigned**, planning their actions in alignment to **operational targets**. Focusing their efforts on **ensuring compliance** to the organizational standards, they **may not look at the bigger picture**. Thus, they may be **less sensitive to the situational demands**, and may not take proactive initiatives. In this scenario, **ownership is only restricted to current duties**, and anticipating the future needs, to meet the expected standards of the management is a challenge. While the team may be able to gauge what is required for the organization's growth, with **low authority**, they may not have the courage to step outside of their comfort zone. Hence, they are likely to be **content with their existing role**, as indicated by their achievement scores. In today's competition, this situation of frog-in-the-well-like attitude could slow down and even make the efforts of the establishment redundant. The group, today, needs to develop the ability to drive change with speed and show willingness to test assumptions. This can help them gain a strategic advantage and anticipate changes.

(Oral Communication + Motivating people + Relationship + Teamwork + Developing People)

Mobilising People – While the group may communicate information related to tasks/projects, and **can motivate the team** to ensure their completion, they may **not focus on developing teams'** repertoire of skills.

Hence, the team would be able to meet immediate expectations, but may find it **challenging to respond to future needs** of a rapidly changing business environment. There also exists a lack of team work, **preventing transparency** and **creating silos**. Impairing work relationships in the process, a spirit of oneness and collaboration may be affected. Hence, while plans are put in place, people are not mobilised, thereby rendering the strategies ineffective.

Testimonials

- "Would like to give the most positive feedback for the assessment-based training session conducted on Tuesday. Taking this experience, I would like to market this kind of team development in our range."

    - Posted By: Mr. Björn Noack Engineering Advanced Technology (DS/EAT-IN), Bosch Limited

- "Thank you for supporting us in the conflict assessment and management workshop. The feedback from the team was extremely positive as they all felt that the assessments gave a different perspective and this session will definitely help them improve their interactions with each other."

    - Posted By: Mr. Dushyant Thomas Head – Human Resources, BorgWarner Cooling Systems

- "We have collaborated with OMi for our assessment, training and developmental needs of the organisation for the last 5 years. OMi synonyms our Training Fulfilment Needs. OMi contributions are laudable with respect to talent development, bringing sea changes in the attitudes and to understand the realistic attributes of our employees. The assessment tools administered by OMi are scientific in nature and the analysis/predictions are accurate. We have extensively used the services of OMi assessment tools for our employee development programs, career planning and also for potential assessment. OMi assessment tools are necessary part of all our training and development programs. We are extremely happy with the analysis, Report and the linkages established in the report with the actual requirements. OMi consultants/Trainers are highly professional, well trained and proactive in their approach and convert complex people issues into feasible solutions through their Training Interventions. Their commitment, involvement and structured feedback to organizations is highly beneficial."

– Posted By: Mr. Venkatesh Kumar A V General Manager – HR & Admin, Buhler

- "OMi was able to bring out the blue print of an individual through psychometric assessments coupled with powerful trainings. The experts pinpoint areas of strengths and weakness and work on it in a customised, focused and periodic manner. The suggestions given were very correct and the company could make use of it to deploy the talent in the right direction. I am really happy to use psychometric analysis in the areas like selection, coaching, career progression, training and effective utilization of resources. It has really added value to organization in terms knowing people better by identifying employee's personality traits, leadership competency, what drives & motivate them, their strengths and areas of improvement."

– Posted By: Mr. Deepak Kumar Sinha Chief Engineer, VOLVO

- "Thank You very much for your Team of professionals on successfully completing Supervisory Development Program – Winning Together – Assessing & Training, for many of our Front-Line Leaders. We appreciate your effort in conducting sessions smoothly & our team members' understanding level was up to mark."

– Posted By: Mr. Gajanan Hegde Asst. Manager. Learning & Development – Dept. HR – Division Toyota Kirloskar Motor Pvt Ltd

- "By taking FITS and other assessments, I get to understand my own strengths and gaps for development. This awareness has given me confidence in my choice of career and focus in developing my gaps. In addition, I also became more objective in my views of others, less emotional. I become more empathetic towards others, and less to expect others to be the same as me. For my staff, I begin to have conversation around their strengths, and what they need for development to fill the gaps. This awareness also helps me to plan more objectively in terms of resources; putting the right people in the right job. I can't say enough of the huge benefits and advantage of understanding these learning. Of course, it is not an overnight learning; it is the continuous support and feedback from the talented coaching from Chinyi and Sreenidhi. It's life skills that all who want to have a fruitful life and a successful career managing people."

– Posted By: Ms. Regina General Sales Manager Haworth North China

• "The assessment and development of our teachers brought about the much-needed self-awareness in all to recognize and initiate attitudinal and behavioural changes. It helped in the modification in oneself towards tapping one's hidden and achieving personal and organisational success."

– Posted by: Dr. Mrs. Stella Samuel Principal Bishop Cotton Girls' School Bangalore